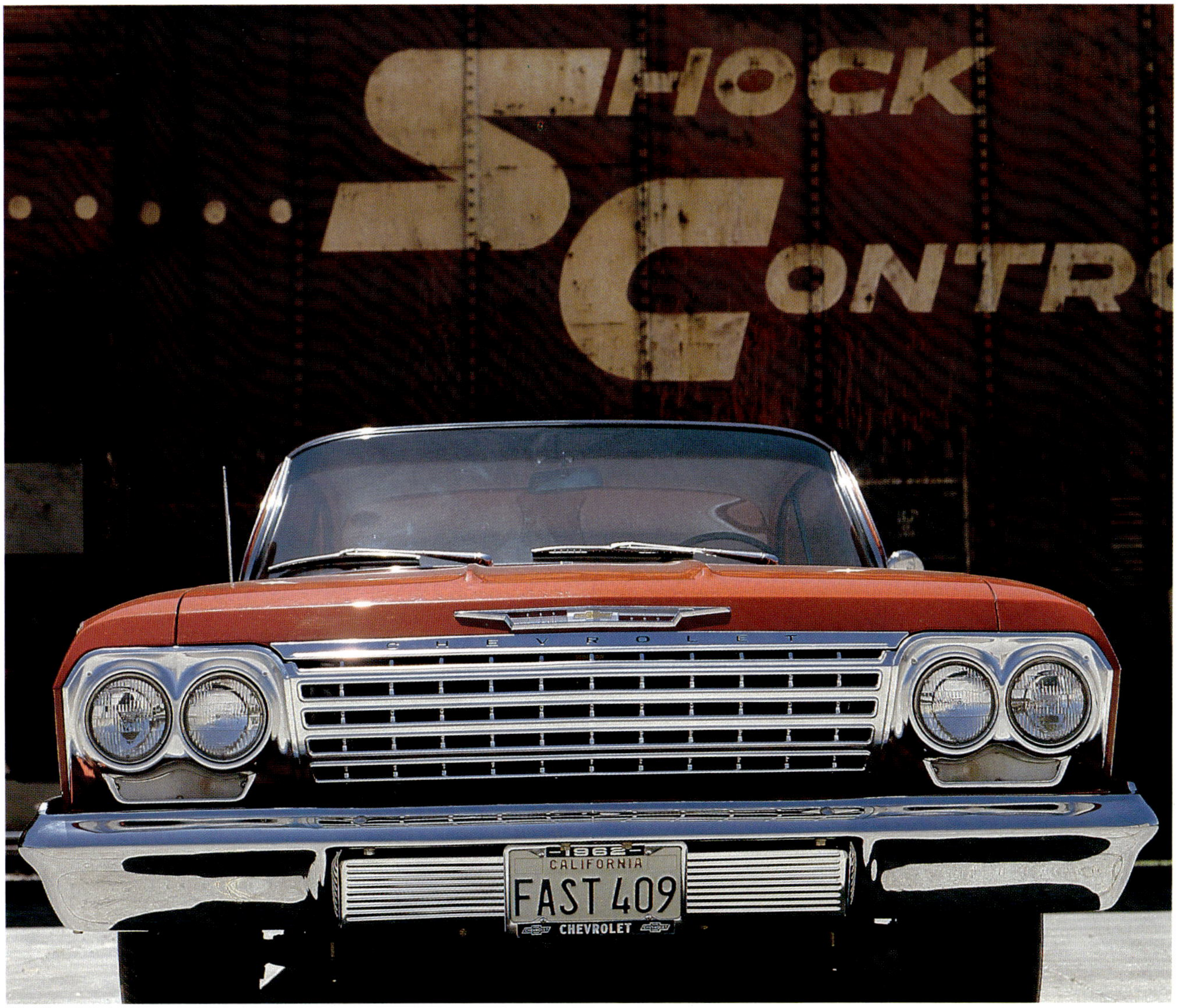
SHOCK
CONTR
CHEVROLET
1962
CALIFORNIA
FAST 409
CHEVROLET

Sixties American Cars
DECADE OF MUSCLE

Henry Rasmussen

Motorbooks International
Publishers & Wholesalers Inc
Osceola, Wisconsin 54020, USA

First published in 1989 by Motorbooks International Publishers & Wholesalers Inc, P O Box 2, 729 Prospect Avenue, Osceola, WI 54020 USA

© Henry Rasmussen, 1989

All rights reserved. With the exception of quoting brief passages for the purposes of review no part of this publication may be reproduced without prior written permission from the publisher

Motorbooks International is a certified trademark, registered with the United States Patent Office

Printed and bound in Hong Kong

The information in this book is true and complete to the best of our knowledge. All recommendations are made without any guarantee on the part of the author or publisher, who also disclaim any liability incurred in connection with the use of this data or specific details

We recognize that some words, model names and designations, for example, mentioned herein are the property of various manufacturers. We use them for identification purposes only. This is not an official publication

Library of Congress Cataloging-in-Publication Data
Rasmussen, Henry
   Decade of Muscle.

   1. Muscle cars—United States—History.
I. Title.
TL23.R38   1989   629.2'222'0973   88-8421
ISBN 0-87938-308-9

Motorbooks International books are also available at discounts in bulk quantity for industrial or sales-promotional use. For details write to Special Sales Manager at the Publisher's address

On the front cover: *The 1970 Mustang Boss 429, the mightiest muscle Mustang.* ***On the back cover:*** *Emblem of an era—Plymouth's winged monster, the 1970 Superbird.* ***On the frontispiece:*** *Face of a muscle car forerunner—Chevy's 409-rigged 1962 Bel Air.* ***On the title page:*** *Possessions of power—the spinner and splitters of a 1964 GTO.* ***On this page:*** *Memorable muscle car metal—the intricate cylinder head of the Hemi.* ***On the next page:*** *Extinct species exposed—the cover comes off a pristine Superbird.*

Contents

Preface   6
Perils of picking and choosing

Introduction   8
Life and times of the muscle car

1962 Chevrolet Bel Air Sport Coupe   20
Most famous of the forerunners

1963 Plymouth Belvedere Max Wedge   28
On the move with the Max

1964 Ford Fairlane Thunderbolt   36
Feathery light and lightning fast

1964 Pontiac LeMans GTO   46
Muscle for the masses

1966 Plymouth Satellite 426 Hemi   56
The Hemi hits the street

1967 Pontiac Firebird 400 HO   64
First of the fire-breathers

1969 Camaro Baldwin Motion Phase III   72
Emergence of a moth-balled missile

1970 Ford Mustang Boss 429   82
Mightiest of the muscle Mustangs

1970 Dodge Challenger R/T 426 Hemi   90
Late-comer captures the laurels

1970 Plymouth Road Runner Superbird   100
Winged monster of NASCAR eminence

1970 Buick Gran Sport GSX Stage I   108
Packing both power and pizzazz

1971 Chevrolet Chevelle SS LS-6   118
Last of the big-blocks turns lean

Preface

Perils of picking and choosing

This book conforms to a standard quota of pages and photographs, as well as a set number of cars to be featured—an even dozen. Consequently, I was faced with the dilemma of choosing the subjects for my camera.

But first, what is a muscle car? Is it just a mid-size automobile, originally designed for the purpose of transporting the average family, but suddenly blessed with a powerful engine and sporty options, and then marketed to a predominantly younger, performance-oriented clientele?

Well, that is a question to ponder.

For the purpose of this book, however, the muscle car is not a sports car, not a two-seater. It is not powered by a small-block engine. And it is not a convertible. Although the open bodystyle is more valuable, it was not used on the drag strip, and that is, after all, where the muscle car originated.

The quintessential muscle car, then, is—and always will be—a 1964 GTO coupe. In my selection, it is flanked by two additional proponents of the original concept: a forerunner, the 1962 Bel Air 409; and a successor, the 1966 Satellite 426 Hemi. These illustrate the optimal contrast between mundane body and macho engine.

Also included are two of the most legendary factory-built drag racers: the Max Wedge and the Thunderbolt.

The pony car is a category unto itself, but the borders are diffuse. Thus, included are examples of the Mustang, Camaro, Firebird and Challenger.

Had I chosen the finalists purely from a viewpoint of performance, they would all have come from 1970. But, for the purpose of providing a historic perspective, just four cars represent this watershed year.

The last gasp of the muscle car era, finally, is exemplified by a 1971 Chevelle SS.

My pick is bound to be controversial; so many worthy candidates had to be left by the roadside. But I am counting on the tolerance of the true enthusiast. After all, we are all in the same boat—or cockpit—all lovers of fast and beautiful machinery.

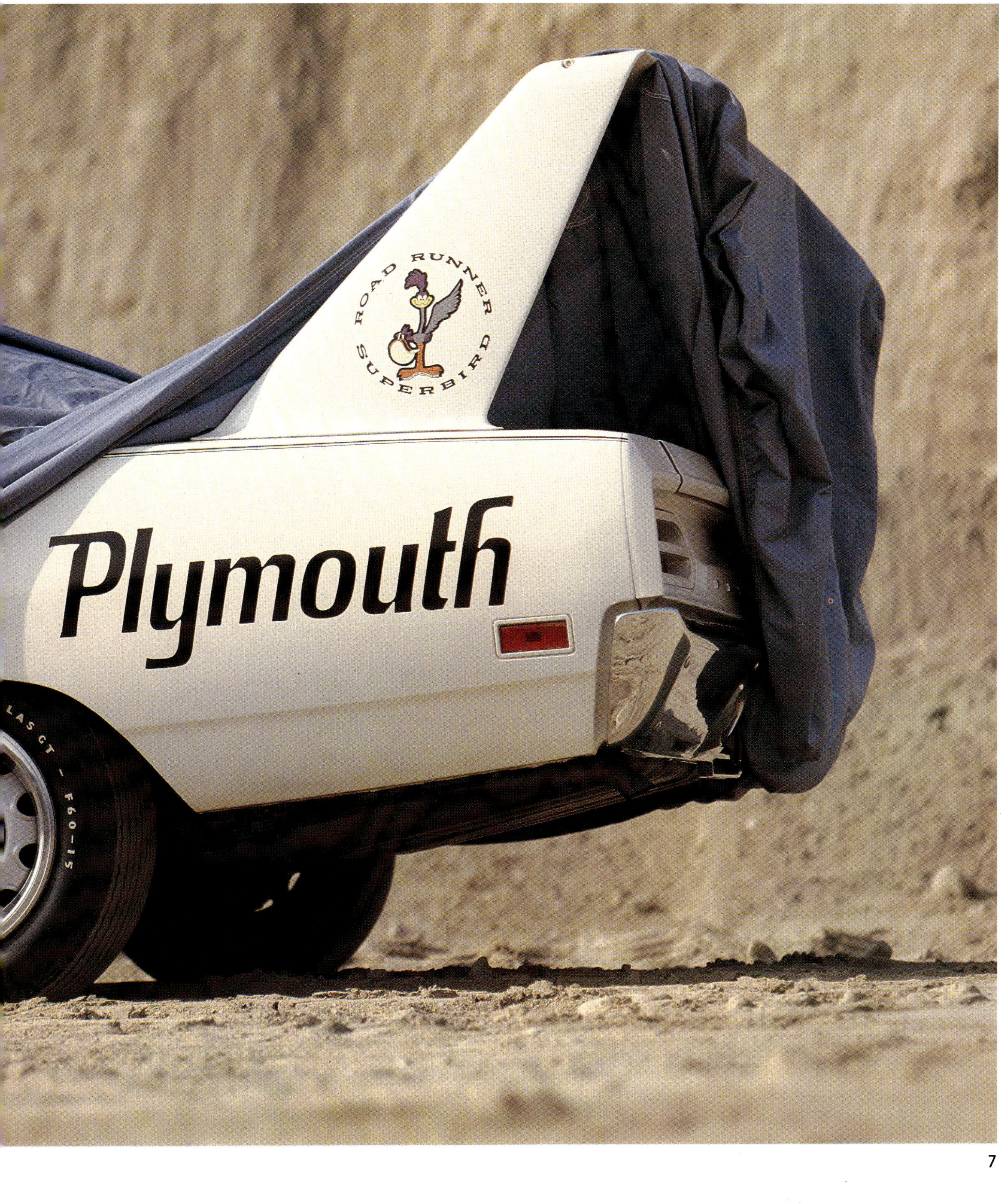
ROAD RUNNER
SUPERBIRD
Plymouth

Introduction

Life and times of the muscle car

"We stand today on the edge of a new frontier...."

When John Kennedy turned the page to the beginning of a new era—ushering in the sixties with these memorable words—a wind of optimism began to sweep the nation. Remember, these were the times of the Peace Corps, America's first space flight and songs like "Days of Wine and Roses."

It was also, more prosaically, a time for the rise of Woodward Avenue, that famed artery growing out of downtown Detroit, passing through Ford, Chevrolet and Chrysler territory, before shooting on toward Pontiac. This was where the pulse of the emerging muscle car era could first be felt. This was the fertile mating ground that gave birth to the GTO.

The fascination with power and speed was not found just locally. The wind of a new age stirred sentiments in every corner of the land. It swept up from the shores of Southern California, where a high school band—calling itself the Beach Boys—conquered the air waves with the immortal line, "She's real fine, my 409...."

The same wind, ripe with the smells of rubber and gasoline, could be felt blasting across the drag strips of Pennsylvania, where daredevils like Dave Strickler and "Dyno" Don Nicholson speed-shifted their way to fame. And it could be seen swooping down over the South, where gladiators like "Fireball" Edward Glenn Roberts and "King" Richard Petty fought it out on the legendary oval at Daytona.

But the optimism of the New Frontier turned abruptly into shock and dismay as the shots in Dallas stopped a nation dead in its tracks. The premature passing of Marilyn Monroe had caused but a temporary pang of pain. A string of assassinations followed that rocked the very foundation of the Great Society, as Malcolm X, Martin Luther King and Robert Kennedy became victims of the escalating pace of social struggle.

Disillusionment was fueled by unrest on campuses across the land. Buttons bearing messages like "We Shall Overcome" and "We Shall Over Kill," illustrated the rift between people, as did bumper stickers advocating "Support Our Boys in Vietnam" and "Make Love Not War." The button "Stoned"

9

suggested a way to escape it all.

It was a time when Cassius Clay became Muhammad Ali. When the Green Berets and Joan Baez stood for opposing expressions of bravery. When films like *In the Heat of the Night* and *Easy Rider* pointed out—each in its own poignant way—the illnesses of the era.

But life had to go on. Beatlemania provided distraction. As did miniskirts. Then, in a change of mood, pantsuits became the "in" thing for the modern woman.

In the midst of it all, flower children continued to blossom, from Haight Ashbury to Woodstock to Greenwich Village. As did the numbers

***T**he excitement never dies—as illustrated on the previous page, where the old drag strip in Carlsbad, California, is revisited by vintage racing action. A 'Cuda, potently equipped with a 440 Six Pack, stands ready to make a roaring run against* the clock. To the right, a 1966 example of The Great One—as in GTO—waits impatiently for its turn. Above, yesteryear's excitement in black and white: 1968 NASCAR racing action livens up the straightaway at Darlington, South Carolina.

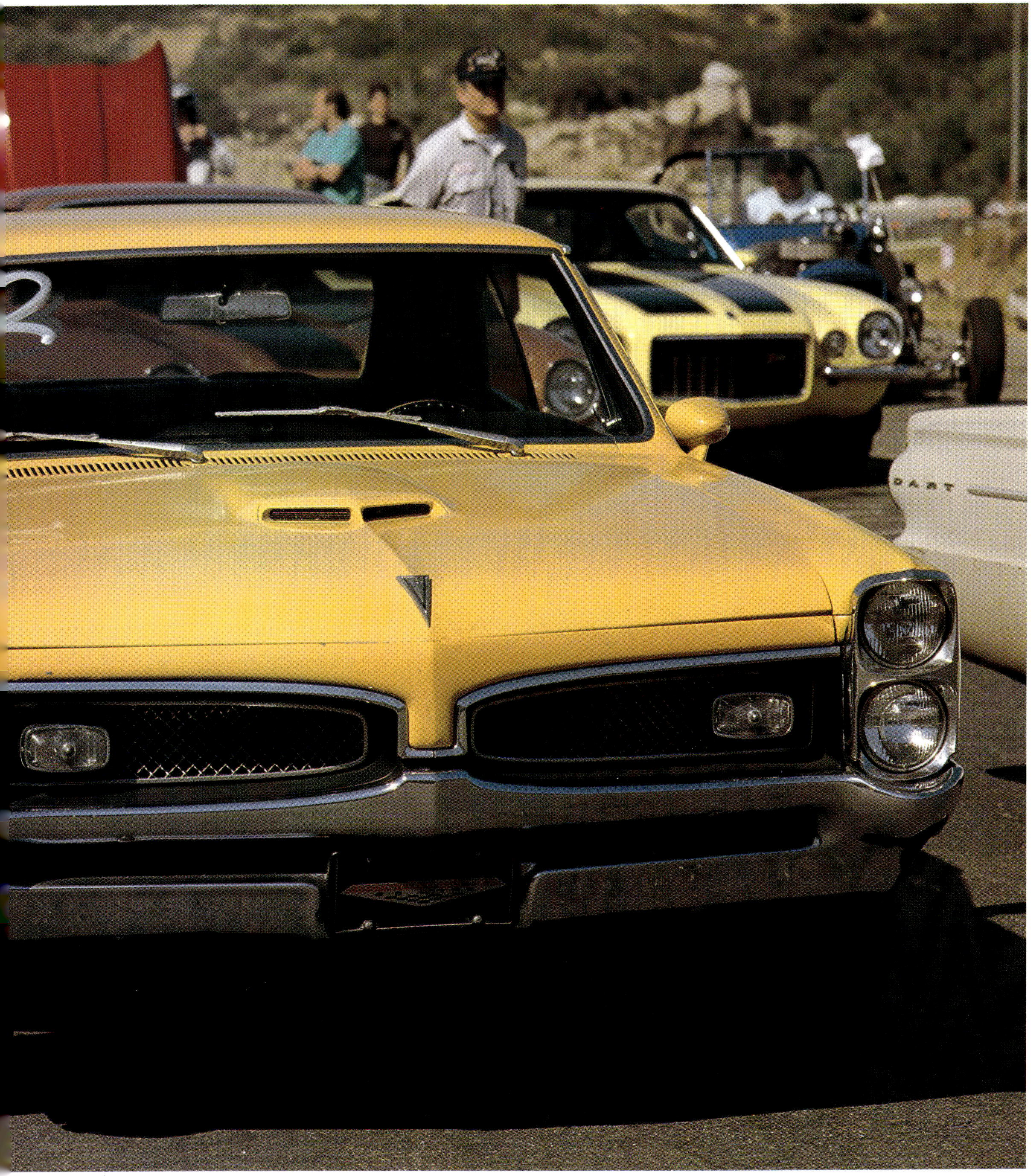
DART

game—the voluptuous measurements of Raquel Welch (37-22-35) vied for attention among other intriguing figures (396, 427, 440). All the while, Johnny Carson made $25,000 per week, Sean Connery $750,000 per movie, and an entry-level Mustang could be had for just 2,368 green ones.

Which brings us back to Detroit and an optimism that just could not be supressed. Nobody wanted the era to end. Nobody—except for that stubborn consumer-rights advocate named Ralph Nader. His book *Unsafe at Any Speed* rubbed the General Motors giant the wrong way. But

Mopars were once the hottest things around, and still are. Above, Richard Petty and his faithful number 43 lead the pack during a 1964 NASCAR battle at Riverside, California. To the right, a Road Runner sporting a special Hemi racing hood and modern Centerline wheels. Decoratively posed against the backdrop of classic drag strip scenery at Carlsbad, the colorful machine makes for more than a pretty picture—it exudes power and confidence in abundance, all in a no-nonsense fashion.

13

nothing seemed to bother Chrysler—the Hemi hit the street, followed by wild, screaming creatures like the Road Runner and the Superbird.

Then came the first real blow. In 1966, the California state legislature passed a bill mandating pollution controls on cars. A year or so later came another shocker. The insurance companies announced the findings of a three-year study on theft and accident levels. The result was a sales-depressing increase in rates. It soon got so bad that the mightiest of the muscle cars became virtually impossible to insure. Then, in late 1971, the rumblings of an impending fuel

Another time, another place—the scene above captures hectic pit action as it looked decades ago. Dick Hutcherson's 1965 Ford gets its bodywork straightened out, as well as a new set of wheels, during that year's Atlanta 400. To the right, other wheels are ready to roll—a 1970 Trans Am with a 400 under the hood stands poised for a duel on the rubber-streaked asphalt. The Pontiac stylists really got the shape right—few nose designs better interpret the look of a snarling beast.

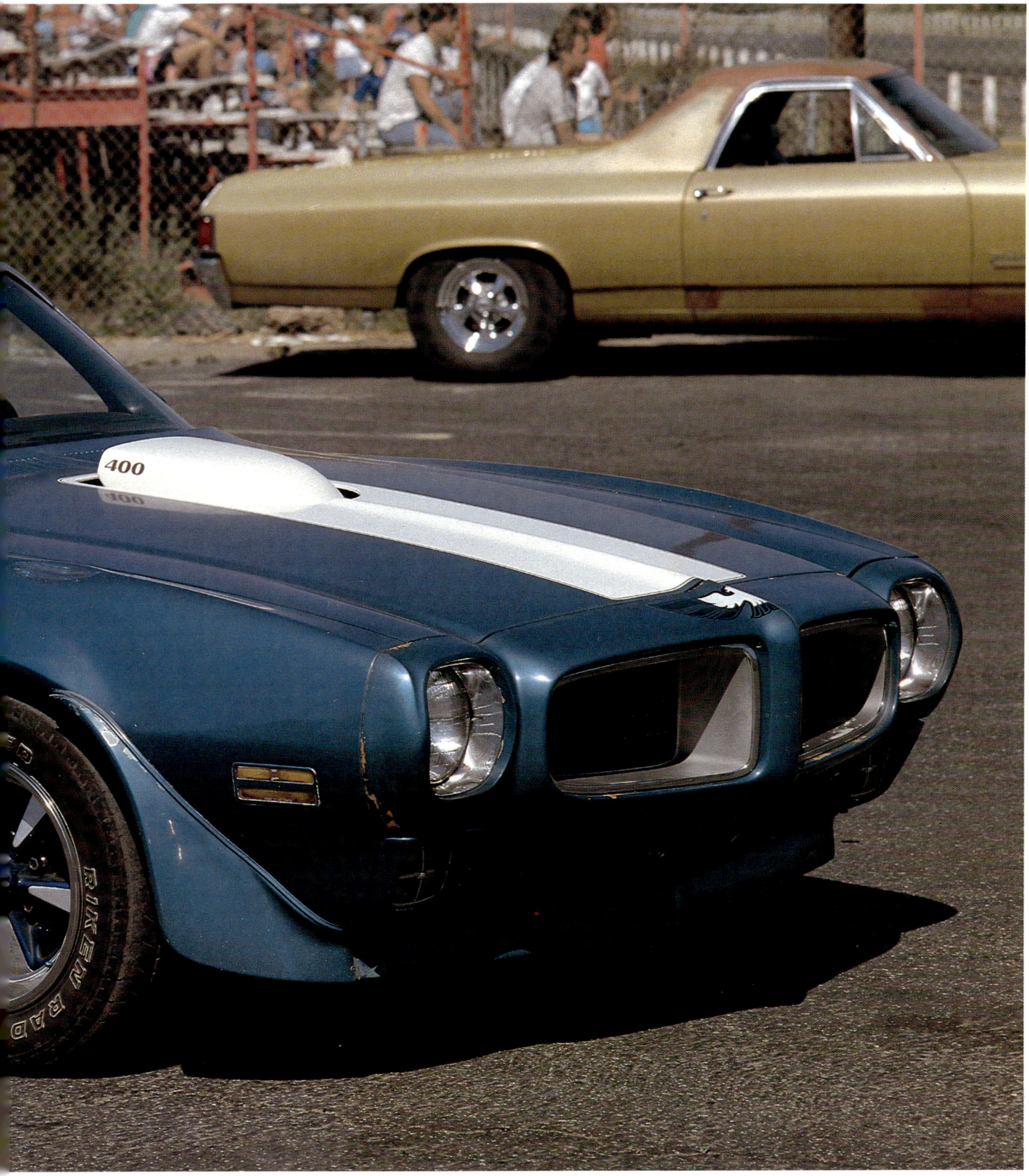
400
RIKEN

crisis sounded a death knell for the muscle car era.

Astronauts Neil Armstrong and Edwin Aldrin planted an American flag on the moon and Richard Nixon pronounced it "the greatest week in the history of the world since creation." But even that did nothing to change the mind of a generation weaned on environmentalist doctrine.

An obscure 1970 notice announced that Anna Thompson Dodge, widow of automotive pioneer Horace E. Dodge, had passed away at the age of 103. It seemed symbolic, somehow. She had lived to see it all—down to the victories and the defeats of the sixties muscle car war. She could take no more. But she died one of the richest women

Clouds of dust and billowing smoke are the compulsive components of all-out muscle car action. Above, Buddy Baker, hot on the heels of Richard Petty, gets his number 3 Dodge Charger squeezed between a rock and hard place when he tries to avoid a couple of out-of-control competitors at Daytona. Fortunately, no injury resulted—nothing that could not be straightened out. To the right, the driver of a Firebird makes good use of the traction compound, creating a spectacular burnout in the process.

17

in the world—rich to the tune of $100 million.

That is somehow the way it ended for us all—rich, not in a monetary sense, but in mementos. For the manifestations of an era when horsepower went haywire—to the chagrin of some, to the enjoyment of others—are still around to be admired. And they are appreciated with a passion, and are appreciating at a pace worthy of an era when outrageous was queen and performance was king.

Studies of muscle cars at speed: above, close-knit action during the 1966 Daytona 500. Plowing its own line through the turn is number 87, an Oldsmobile Toronado, piloted by Buck Baker. Trying to squeeze by on the inside is number 93, a 1964 Ford, reined by Blackie Watt. Number 56, a 1965 Plymouth, driven by Jim Hurtubise, is biding its time in the draft behind the leader. Pictured to the right, more action at the Carlsbad drag strip. A 1970 Ford Torino is so quick off the mark that it leaves a blur in its wake.

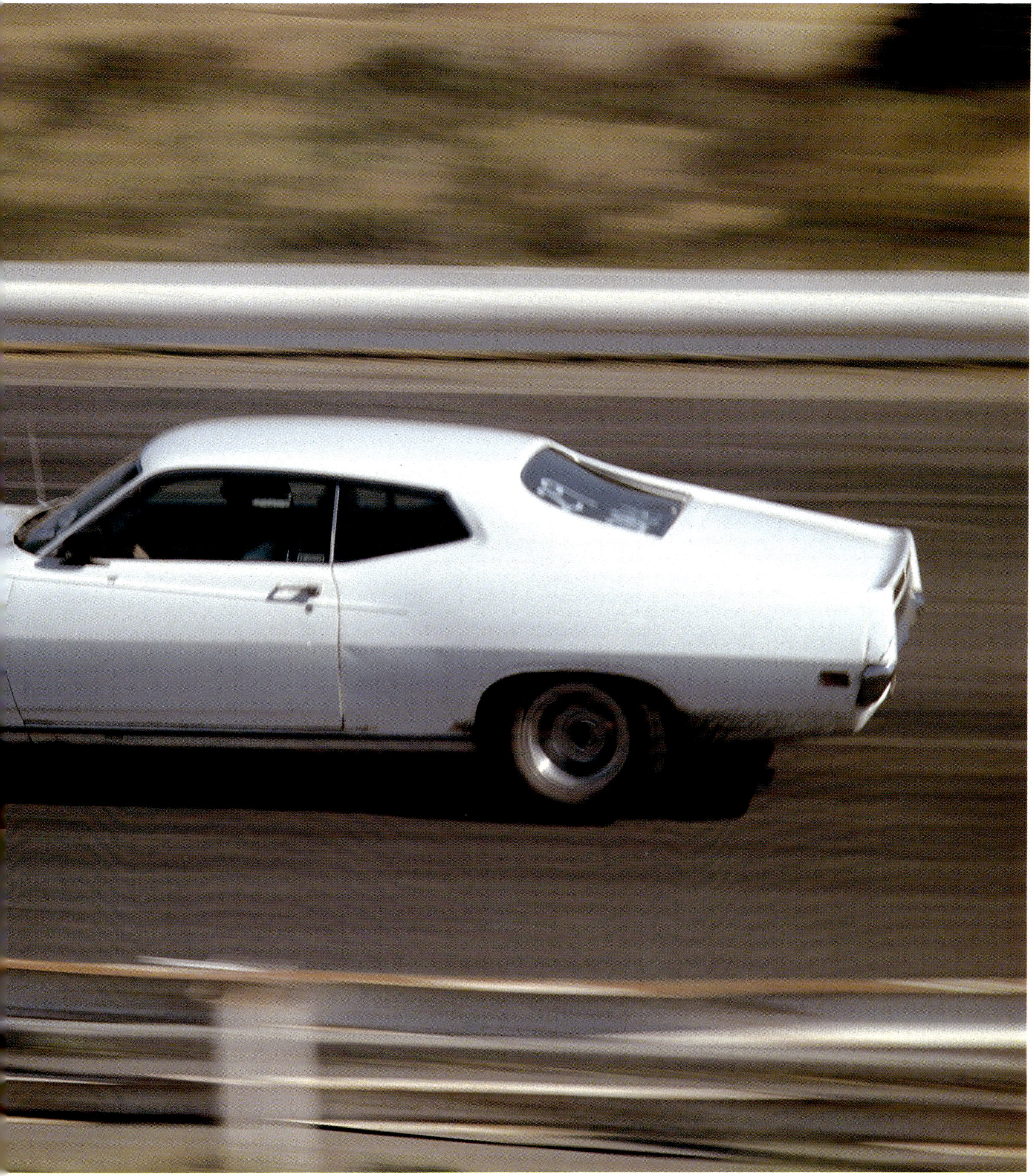

1962 Chevrolet Bel Air Sport Coupe

Most famous of the forerunners

"*S*he's real fine, my 409...."

In the early sixties the war for domination of the nation's drag strips and racetracks—as well as its streets—reached a crucial stage, forcing the auto makers to up the ante once again.

The horsepower showdown was certainly not a new phenomenon. In the fifties, first Oldsmobile, then Hudson, had made a name for themselves—and impressive sales gains—by excelling on the racetrack.

A new generation saw the fight spill over to the streets with increasing ferocity. When this happened, Chevrolet found itself outclassed. Fortunately, the Chevrolet engineers had a lethal weapon in the works—the 409, put into limited action in 1961.

Pontiac's GTO is proclaimed as the machine that sparked the muscle car explosion. In the sense that this design embodied the specific combination of power, looks and price to first catch the fancy of the masses, its place in muscle car history is indisputable. But all trends have forerunners—and Chevrolet's Bel Air Sport Coupe, fitted with the 409 option, is the most famous of these early machines.

The 409 motor was the ultimate development of the division's workhorse W-series 348. In 1961, breathing through a single four-barrel Carter, the engine developed 360 hp, and found its way into a limited number of Impala Super Sports.

For 1962, the addition of a second carburetor produced a neat parity—the 409 now sported 409 horses. Approximately 15,000 such units were mated to Impalas, Biscaynes and Sport Coupes when this hot new item was made available as an option in the three Chevrolet models offered that year.

Of these, the Sport Coupe was the model chosen by drivers with a serious intent. This preference was mainly due to the shape of the roof, which had been held over from the previous year, after tests had shown that Chevrolet's new roofline for 1962 had an unfavorable effect on aerodynamics.

Close to 6,000 Sport Coupes are thought to have been built, but no accurate figure can be obtained, since the manufacturer did not keep records of the particular combination of models and engines.

Although Chevrolet had officially stayed away from competition since 1957, the manufacturer still retained a department catering to the all-out racer. It is said the organization was so secret not even top brass were aware of its existence.

With unofficial encouragement from this clandestine group at Chevrolet, specially prepared 409 Sport Coupes reached the pinnacle of drag strip fame in 1962. One of these winners was campaigned by Californian Hayden Proffitt, who ran a most impressive season, ultimately capturing the national championship in the Super Stock division.

Proffitt's bright red machine, sporting the slogan "Just 4 Chevy Lovers" on its sweeping side panels, was powered by a highly massaged unit, thought to produce close to 500 horses. This blockbuster of an engine was capable of propelling the slippery Sport Coupe down the quarter-mile strip at a shattering clip, stopping the watches somewhere in the mid-twenties.

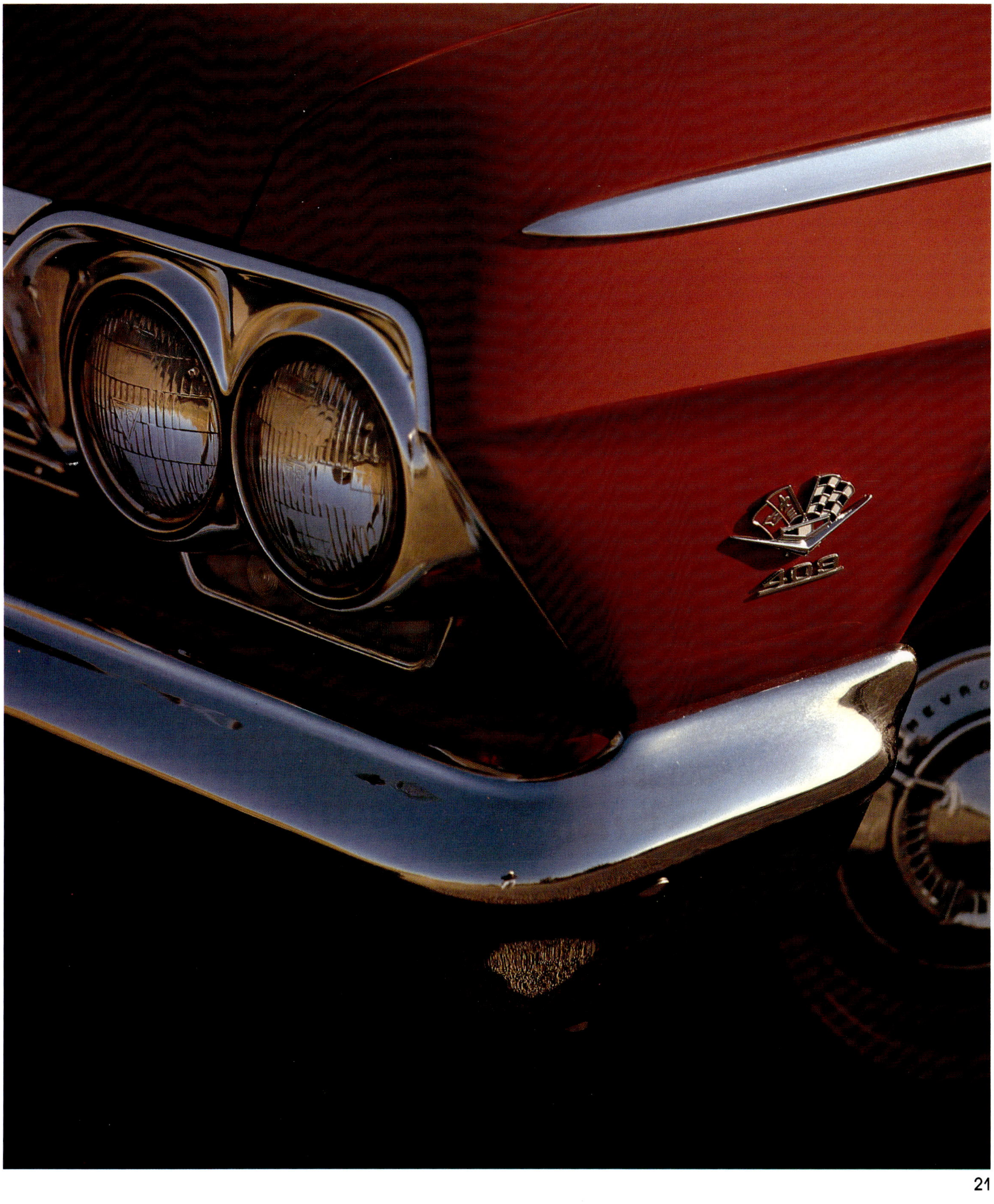
409

*T*he sight of the cross-flag emblem in combination with the 409 numerals—on the previous page—was enough to stir excitement on the street as well as on the drag strip. The Bel Air Sport Coupe of 1962—pictured here and on the following page—perpetuated the basic look of the previous year, when the model made its debut sporting an Impala badge on the rear fender. The grille still incorporated twin headlight assemblies, but was updated in accordance with Chevrolet's general trend for the model year. Also changed was the molding on the side panel. Wide in 1961, it had now become a subtle chrome strip, running the full length of the body. In this form, the model lasted just one year. The particular example featured here was campaigned by drag racer Tom Sturm. In its heyday the potent survivor made life extremely tough for fellow racers on drag strips all across Southern California.

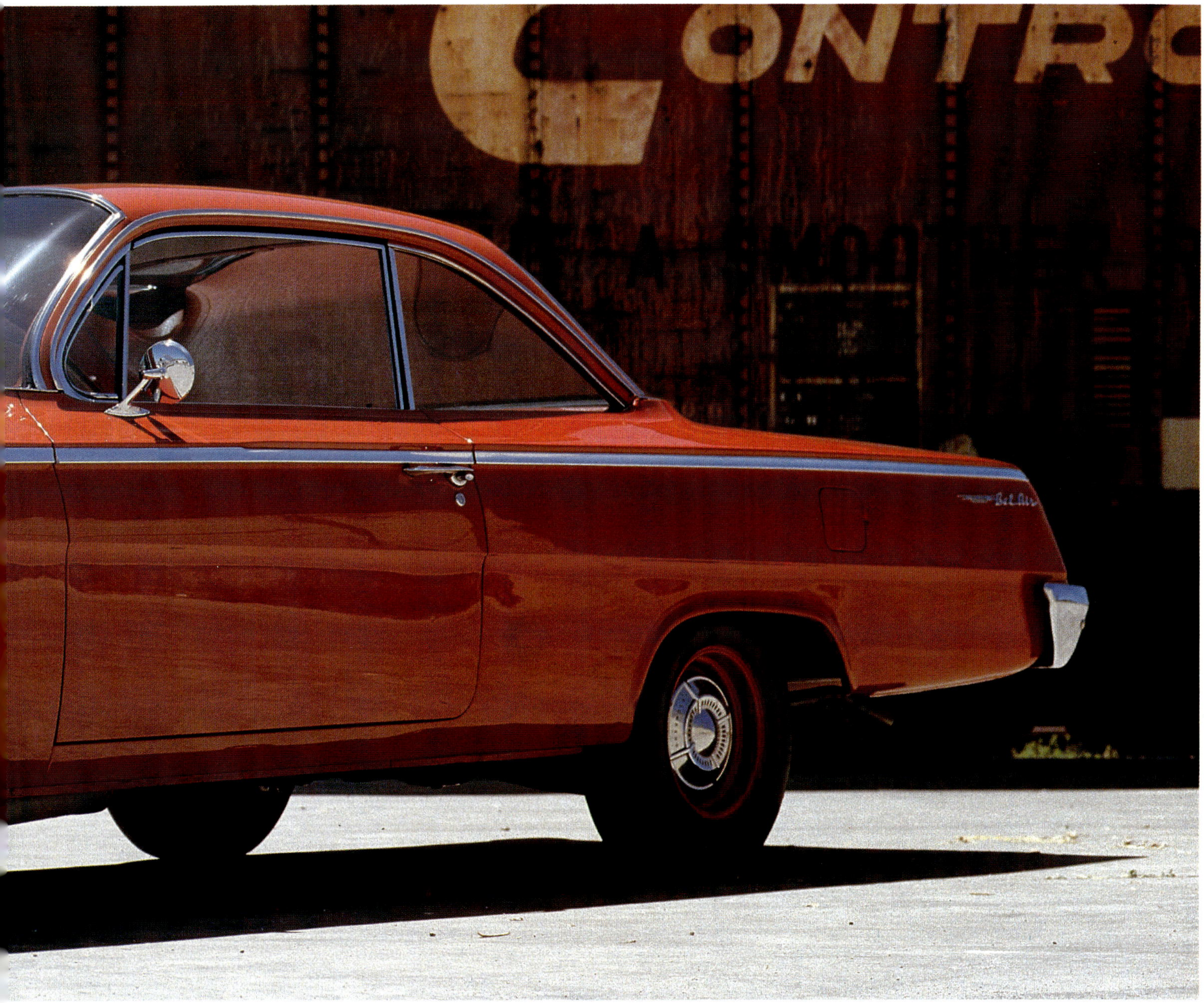
CONTR

DF
....with
UNDERFRAM
CHEVROLET
Bel Air
1962
SEP CALIFORNIA
FAST 409
CHEVROLET

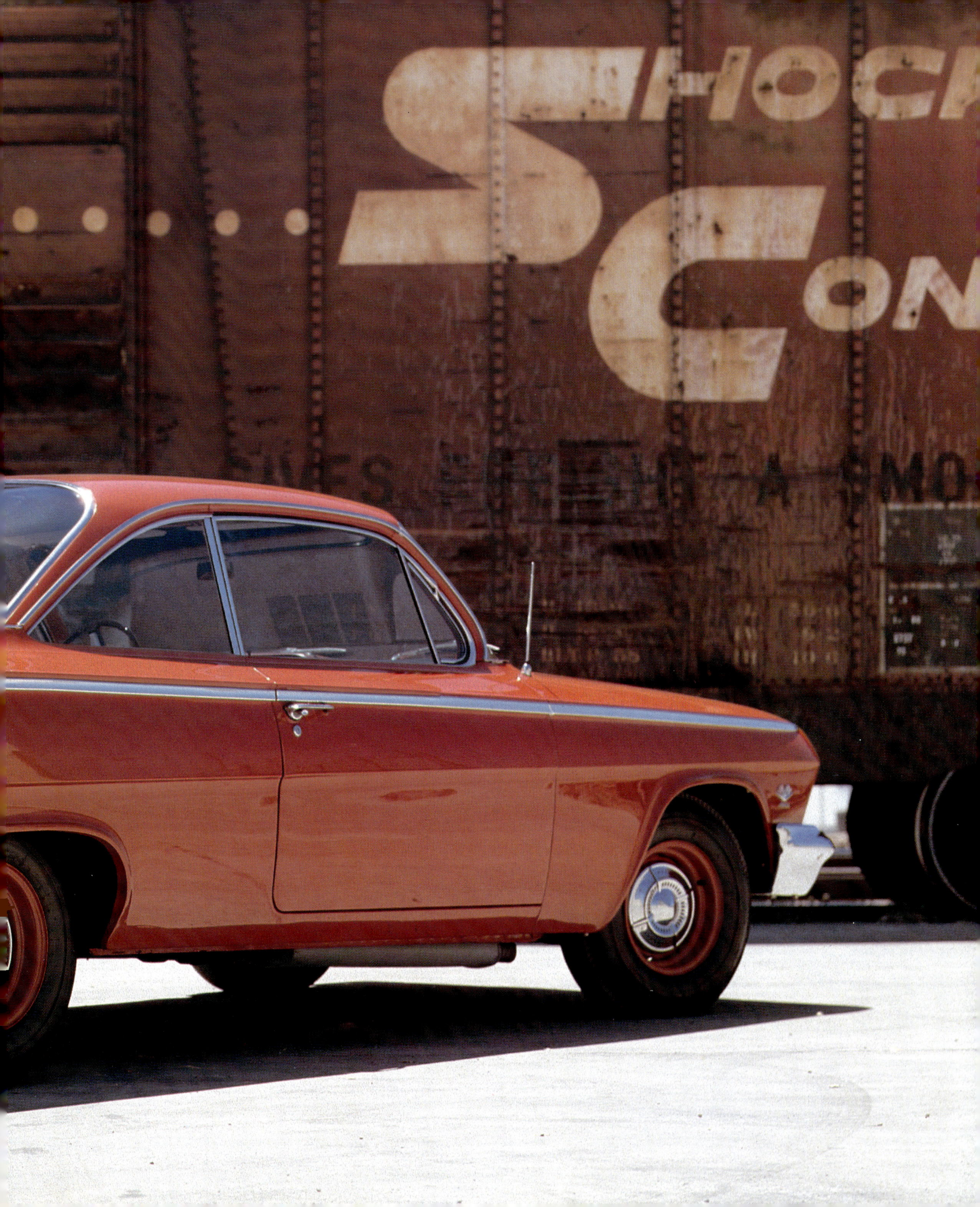

The cause of all the commotion here, the 409 Turbo-Fire engine. This photograph shows the stock configuration, where two four-barrel Carters were virtually hidden by the air cleaner. The power peak was reached at 6200 rpm. On the track version, lightweight components allowed the 409 to reel off in excess of 7000 rpm. To the right, the Bel Air interior. Two details indicate that this machine is not run-of-the-mill: the floor-mounted shift lever and, partly obscured by the steering column, the tachometer. Instrumentation and interior otherwise remained the same as on the standard Bel Air, including the front bench seat, which, together with the back seat, offered ample space for six occupants. A full load naturally slowed acceleration, but true to the concept of the muscle car, the Bel Air—weighing in at a respectable 3,300 pounds—covered the quarter-mile in just over 15 seconds. All this at a cost of just $2,561, plus $484 for the Turbo-Fire package.

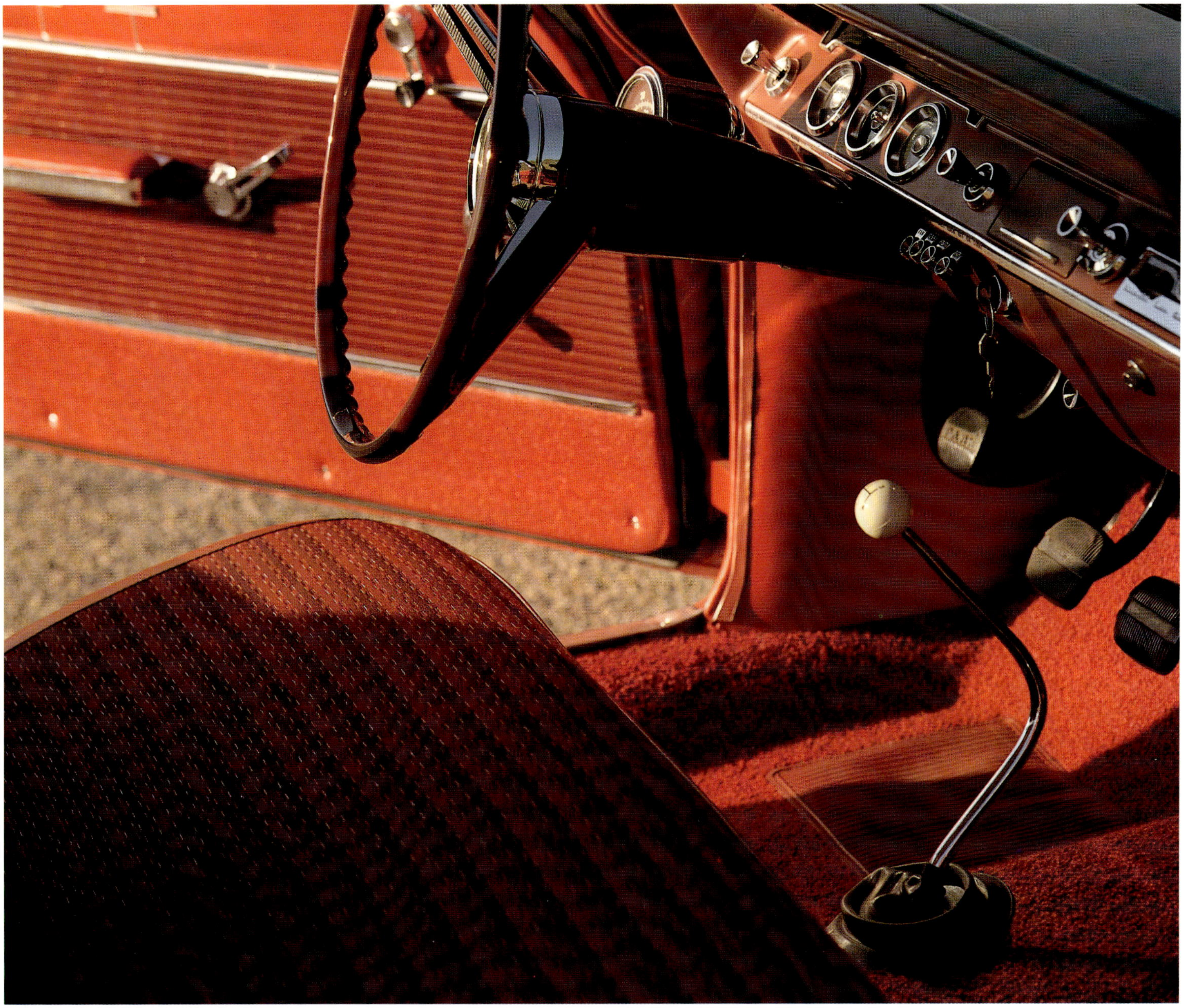

1963 Plymouth Belvedere Max Wedge

On the move with the Max

The Super Stock 426 in all its glory.

Automotive fortunes, like the stock market, seem to be one of those things you can count on to fluctuate. Plymouth, for instance, after having a good year in 1960, with a total production of nearly half a million units, saw the number of registered cars plummet to below the 300,000 mark in 1961—a low the manufacturer had not experienced since 1946.

Something had to be done to prevent the marque—which had been around since 1928—from being swept away with the outgoing tide. The recipe for recovery contained a three-pronged strategy—new styling, improved warranty and image enhancement through racing.

For 1962, Plymouth unveiled its "New Forward Flair Design." Even though a slogan asked the public to "Look at Plymouth Now!" matters hardly improved. In 1963, the manufacturer announced its five-year or 50,000-mile warranty. Styling was changed again. And the equation finally seemed to work—425,000 units were registered. Helping things to move in the right direction was the slogan "Get up and go Plymouth!"

The 1963 line consisted of the entry-level compact Valiant. The lowest priced of the Plymouths, it started at $1,973 and came equipped with a 171 ci, 101 hp six-cylinder engine. The Savoy was the least expensive full-size Plymouth, starting at $2,262. Power still came from a six-cylinder unit, displacing 225 ci and producing 145 hp. Also available was a V-8, measuring 317 ci and generating 230 hp.

Next in the line-up came the Belvedere. It was available with the same six-cylinder unit used in the Valiant, or with the V-8 fitted to the Savoy. At the top of the line were the Fury and the Sport Fury. Although also available with six-cylinder units, it was the optional V-8 versions—318 Commando, 383 Golden Commando and 426 Super Stock II Commando engines—that generated interest among performance people.

Another slogan from 1963 was "Plymouth's On The Move." This terse, confidence-filled statement undoubtedly took its cue directly from the manufacturer's impressive performance on the racetrack. Responsible for this new vitality was the fabulous 426 Wedge motor, originally put into service when the first-generation Hemi became too costly to build.

The Wedge, like the Hemi, derived its name from the shape of the combustion chambers. Available as a little-known option in the Belvedere line, expressly for the buyer with racing in mind, the Wedge produced an ample measure of muscle. When this formidable unit was coupled to Plymouth's three-speed, tough-as-nails TorqueFlite transmission and placed into a specially lightened Belvedere—called the Max Wedge—it became the combination to beat on the drag strips. Cars with the Wedge finished first and second in USAC (United States Auto Club) racing. And, on the NASCAR (National Association for Stock Car Racing) circuit, Richard Petty began to make a name for himself—and Plymouth.

The recovery recipe worked. For 1964, total production swelled to almost 600,000, and remained high throughout the muscle car era.

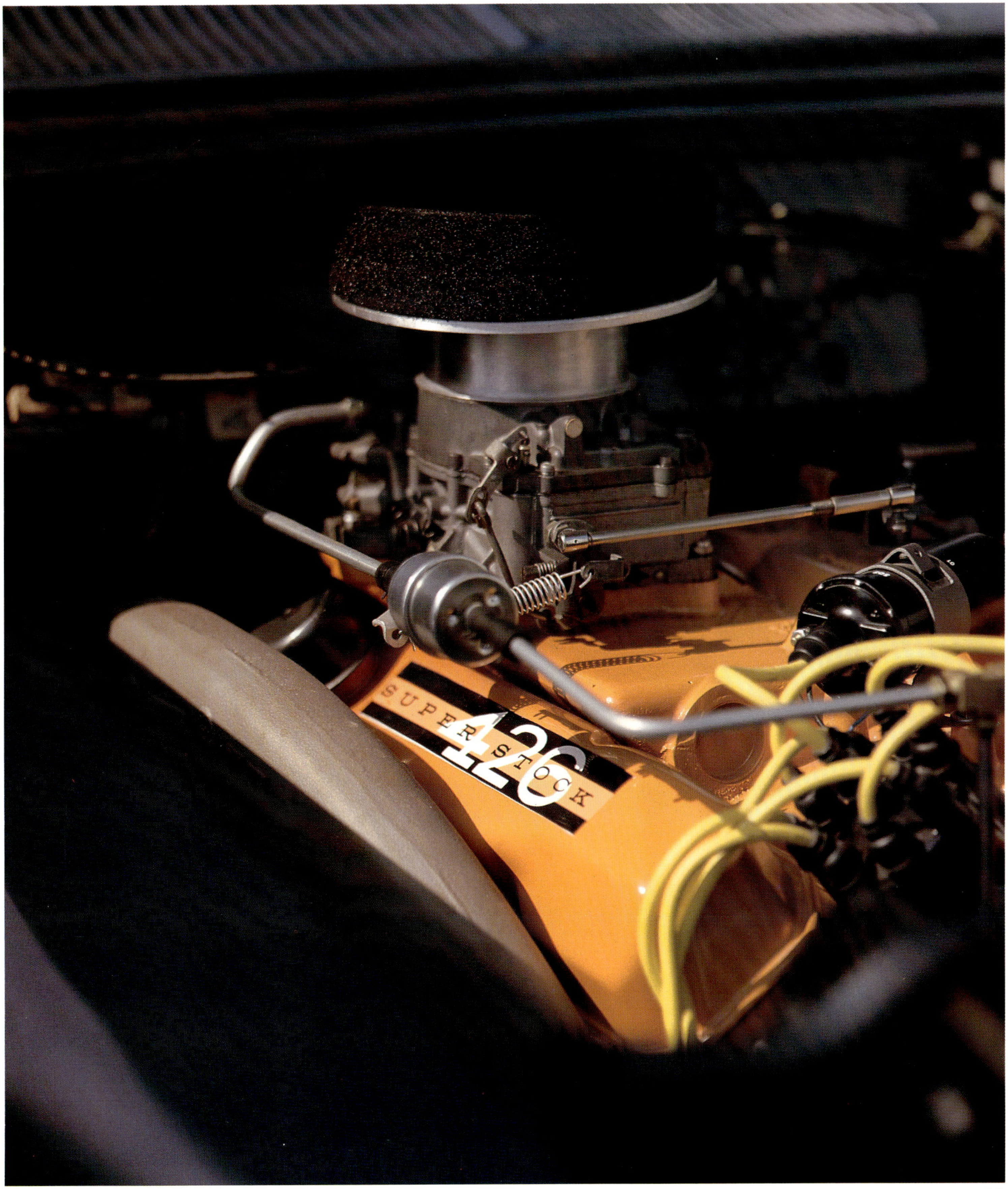
SUPER STOCK
426

The Max Wedge was based on Plymouth's middle-of-the-road Belvedere—a new design for 1963. The most eye-catching of the styling details were the tall directional lights, mounted vertically in each corner of the front fenders. Plymouth's Max, as opposed to Ford's Thunderbolt, was built in-house. A Belvedere was taken right off the assembly line and fitted with fenders, hood and under-bumper aluminum valance. Topping this lightweight assembly—which saved about 150 pounds—was a hood scoop, also manufactured from aluminum. About 210 Max Wedges are thought to have been built. The particular car featured here was once a full-fledged competitor, seen often at the Northern California Fremont drag strip, where it ran for the last time as recent as 1967. Known as the Panic Button, the machine—now restored to its stock appearance—was capable of covering the quarter-mile in just over 12 seconds.

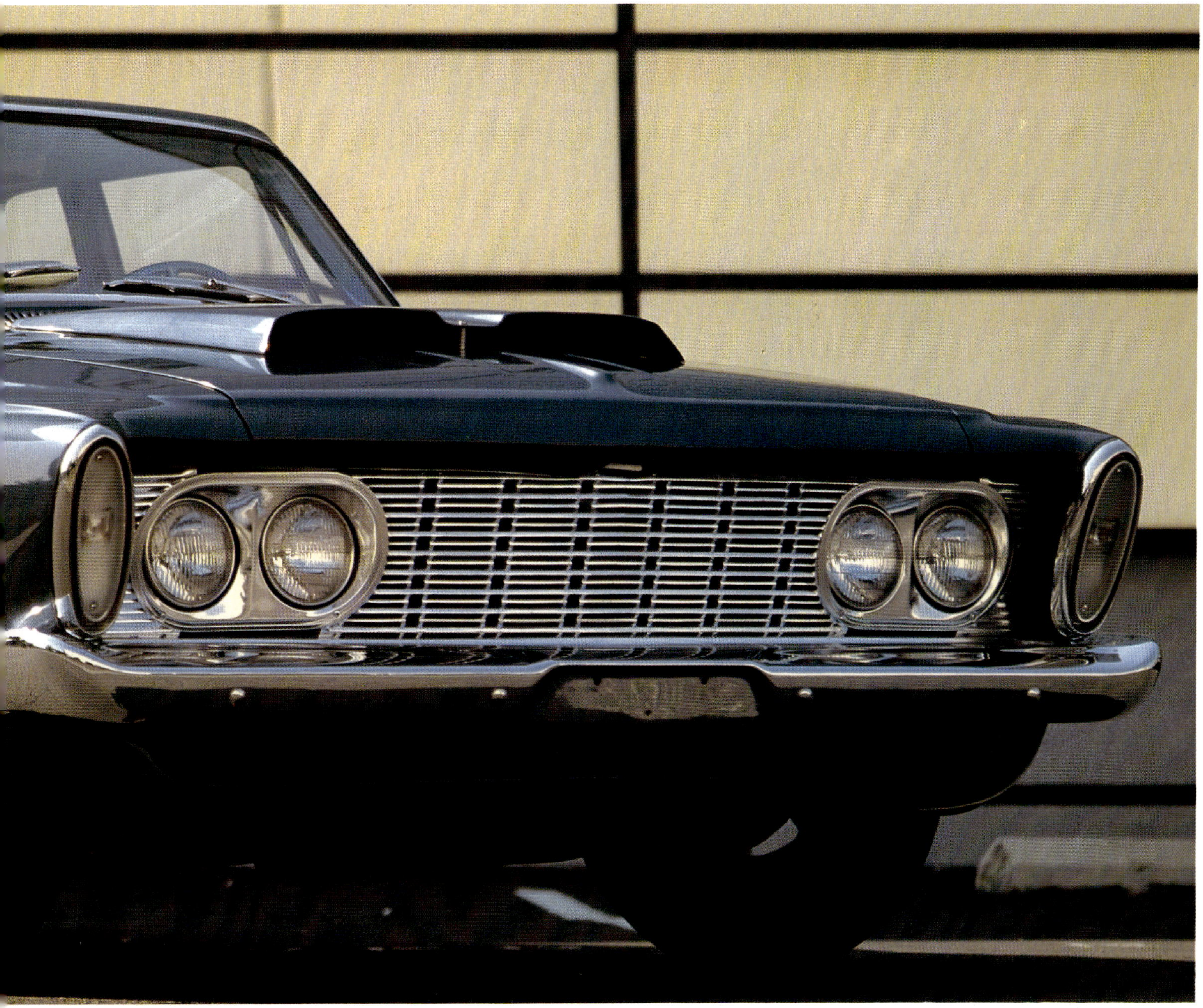

HANDS OFF *Aluminum!*

SUPER 426 STOCK

The Super Stock Wedge displaced 426 ci and produced 425 hp at 5600 rpm. The compression ratio was 13.5:1. Twin four-barrel Carters—as shown here—were mounted on top of Chrysler's patented ram-type manifold. A 3.5 inch velocity stack was added to the rear carburetor, and a 2.5 inch unit to the forward one. These raised the air cleaners to the level of the hood scoop. Two-inch foam rubber rings were used to facilitate the sealing. There were no heat ports, so the Wedge had to be properly warmed up before it would run well. The picture on the opening pages of this chapter provides a closer look at the rear Carter, as well as the left cam cover with its "426 Super Stock" decal—replaced by a remanufactured unit during the restoration. Immediately to the left of the cover is a swooping portion of the cast-iron exhaust manifold, which dumped into huge four-inch pipes—the Max did nothing to hide its true purpose.

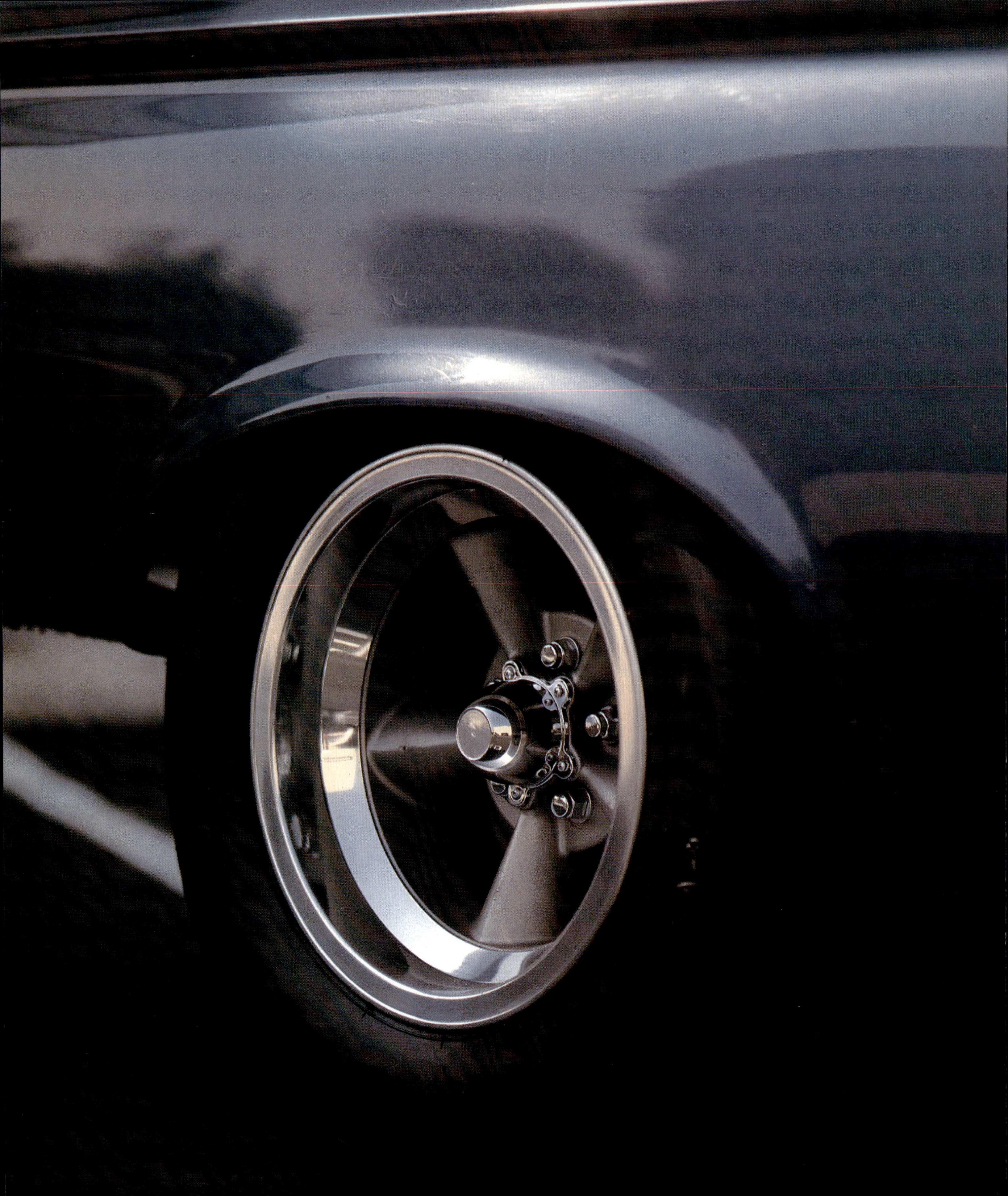

To the left, the Max Wedge was fitted with rear rubber that seemed to fill the wheelwell—to the max. A Chrysler station wagon provided the seven-inch rims, which were wrapped with wide 9/14 size tires. The front featured a standard six-inch Belvedere wheel, sporting narrower 750/14 tires. The interior, above, was lightened through the removal of radio and heater, and the floor covered with a no-nonsense rubber mat. The featured car sports a Sun tachometer, mounted in the middle, right on top of the steering column. This item, curiously, was not included in the Max Wedge package as delivered from the factory, but was fitted by the dealer or the individual racer. Also missing is an oil pressure gauge. The super-competent Torqueflite transmission was a factory-modified heavy-duty version, and was operated via dash-mounted push buttons.

1964 Ford Fairlane Thunderbolt

Feathery light and lightning fast

Seldom seen—Thunderbolts square off.

During the course of the 1963 drag racing season, it became painfully evident to Ford that its Galaxies did not have what it took to deliver the knock-out punch to the ferocious Plymouths. It was not so much a lack of power as it was a matter of too much weight—the Plymouths, with their unit-body construction, had the Fords beaten already on the scales.

The solution was to shoehorn the 427 into the smaller and lighter Fairlane. This mid-size model, measuring 115.5 inches between front and rear wheels, had a three-inch advantage over the Galaxie. Through the use of fiberglass panels where feasible, the weight was reduced further—to just over 3,200 pounds. This precisely matched the formula set forth by the NHRA (National Hot Rod Association), 7.5 pounds per cubic inch at a seven-liter displacement limit.

The competitors involved in the actual battle on the track were sometimes ahead of the factory engineers when it came to realizing the need and how to achieve it. This was indeed the case with the Thunderbolt. It was Bob Tasca—a Ford dealer in Providence, Long Island, and the power behind a successful drag racing team—who pioneered the use of the Fairlane.

Tasca had displayed the possibilities of this combination during the latter part of the 1962 season, and his subsequent successes finally opened the eyes of the Ford executives. An order was placed with Andy Hotton's Dearborn Steel Tubing for fifty-seven units, following the general specifications set forth by Tasca. Popular demand added another forty-three units to the total number of Thunderbolts built. Thus was born one of the most celebrated drag strip stars of the era.

The first Thunderbolts went to established Ford racers such as "Gas" Gaspar Ronda, Les Ritchey, Phil Bonner, Dick Brannan and, of course, the Bob Tasca team. At the 1964 season-opening Winternationals, Ronda—who had begun his career as a part-time drag racer while still working as a full-time dance studio instructor—managed to beat the competition to capture the Super Stock stick class. He went on to finish the season as the winner of the national championship title.

When first taking delivery of his Thunderbolt, Ronda ran the quarter-mile at 12.2. During the course of the season, he lowered his time to 11.9. And later forced it even lower, to 10.9.

With the Thunderbolt being produced specifically for the purpose of racing, Ford was careful to inform the buyer of this fact. A plaque, attached to the inside of the glove compartment lid, spelled out Ford's disclaimer in no uncertain terms. In addition, before taking delivery, the owner had to sign a document acknowledging that the machine was not covered by any warranty.

It has been said that each Thunderbolt cost Ford more than $6,000. With a sticker of $3,900—and an additional $100 for the automatic—the financial equation only made sense when consideration was given to the public relations value. It was certainly a small price to pay for fame.

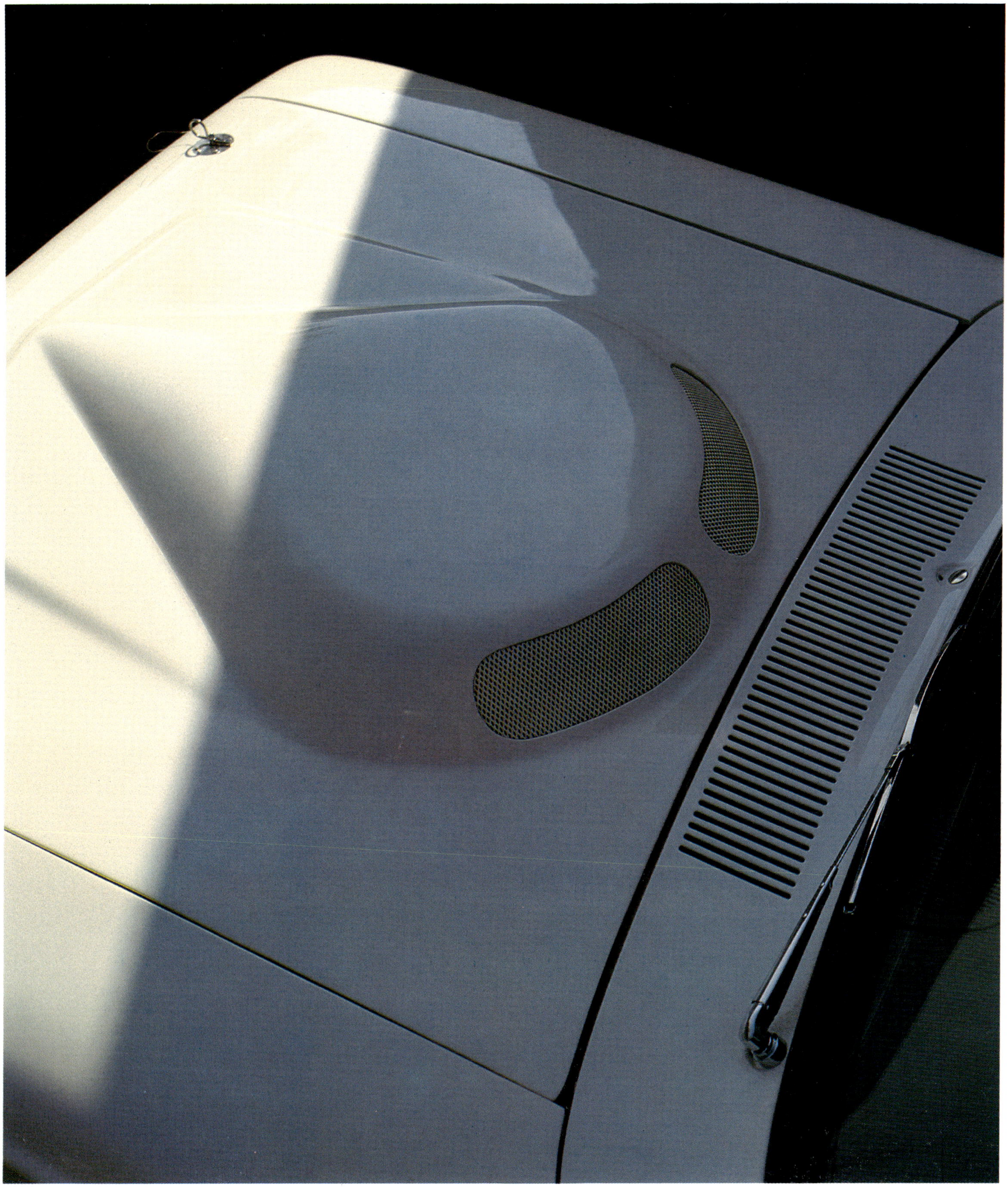

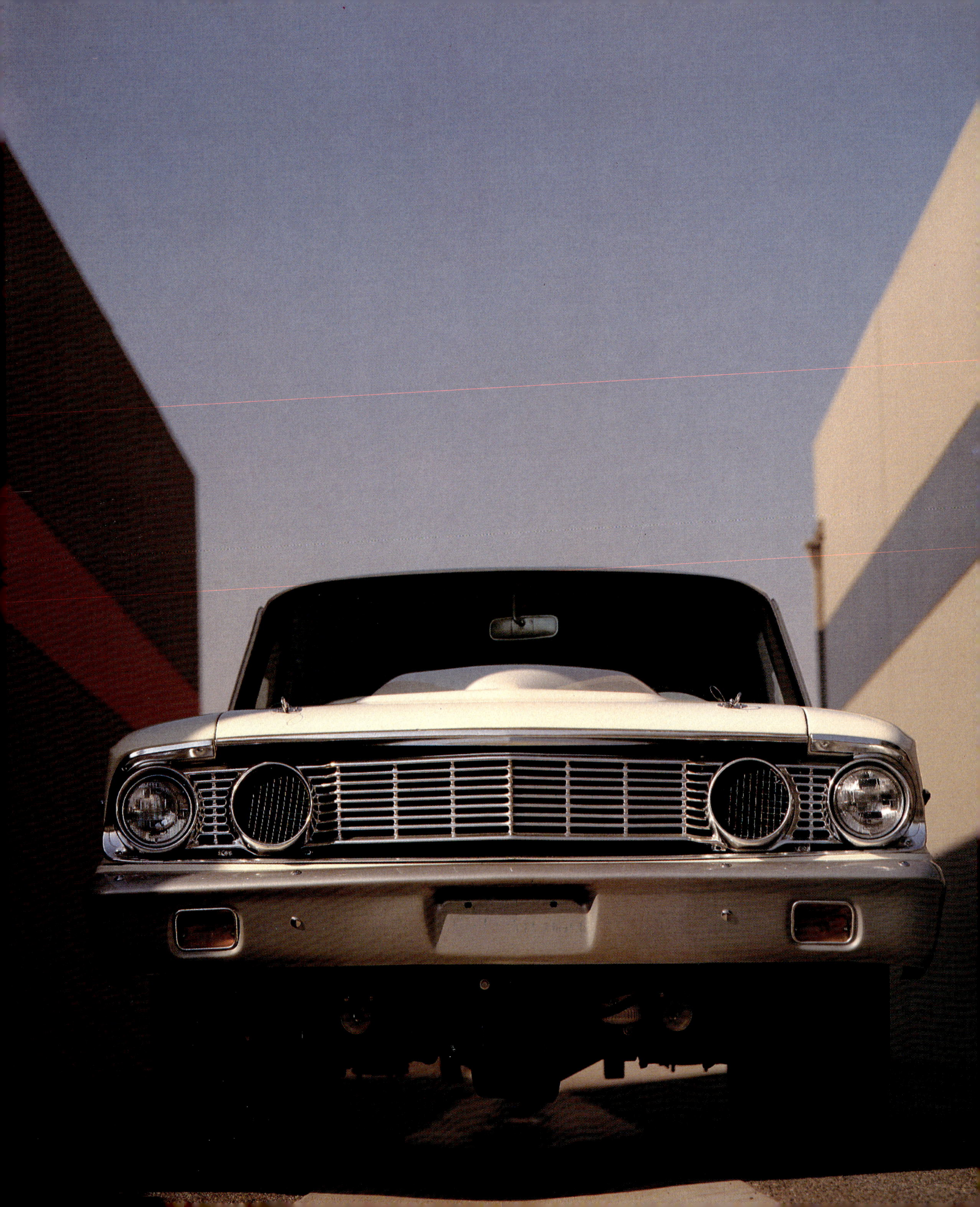

The Thunderbolt used fiberglass for the hood, front fenders and doors, as well as the front bumper—although later units were fitted with aluminum bumpers. The photograph on the chapter opening page shows a bird's-eye view of the teardrop-shaped hood blister—a feature that subsequently became something of a trademark of the racing Fords. Here, two views of a front end that advertises its down-to-business racing purpose like an animal's intent to attack. The following photograph captures the full view of the machine that became such a familiar sight in the winner's circle. It is surprising to note that the weight-saving measures did not include the removal of the chrome spear from the side panel. It was obviously more important to retain identification with the cars in the showrooms. After all, increased sales were the obvious purpose for the manufacturer's involvement with racing.

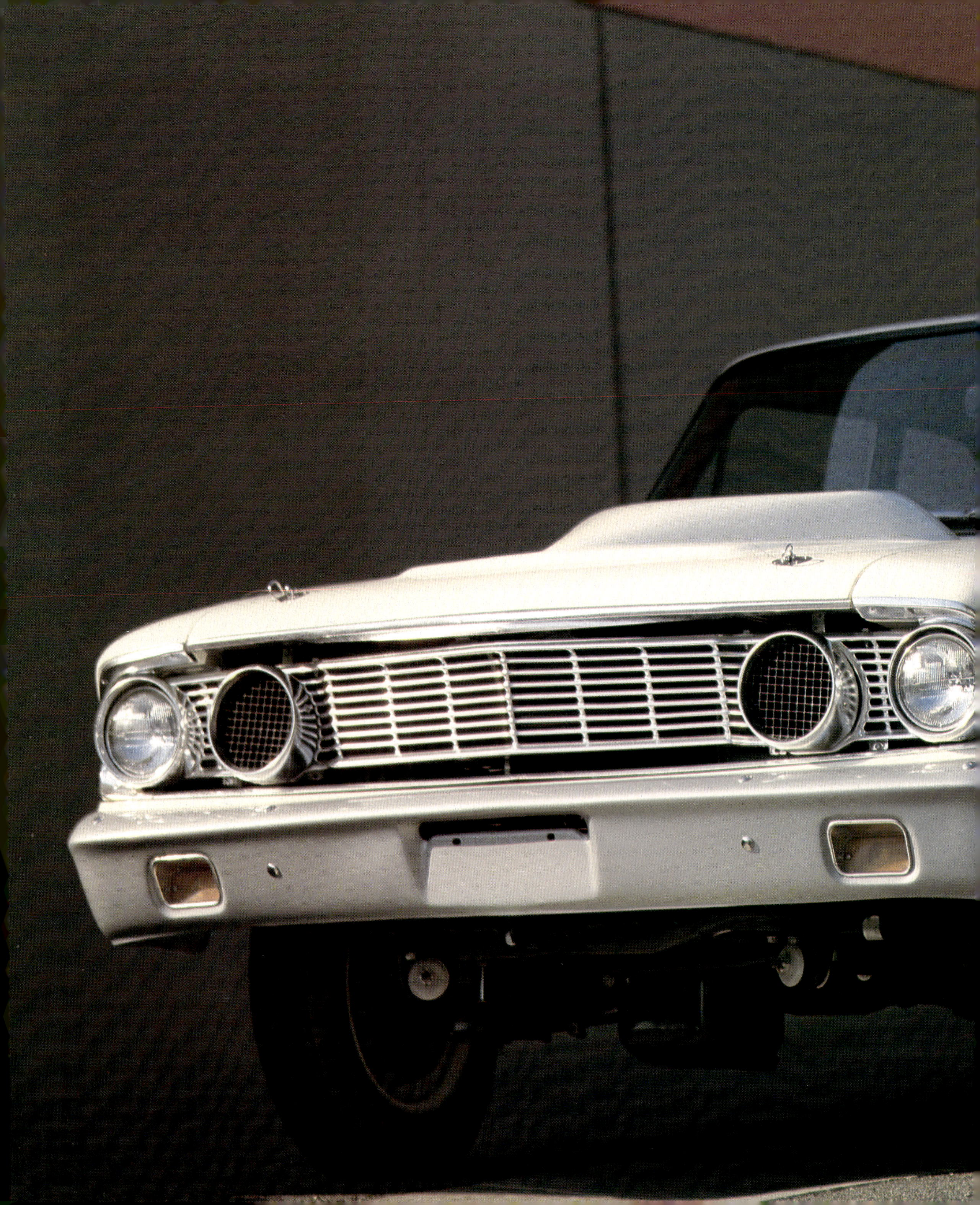

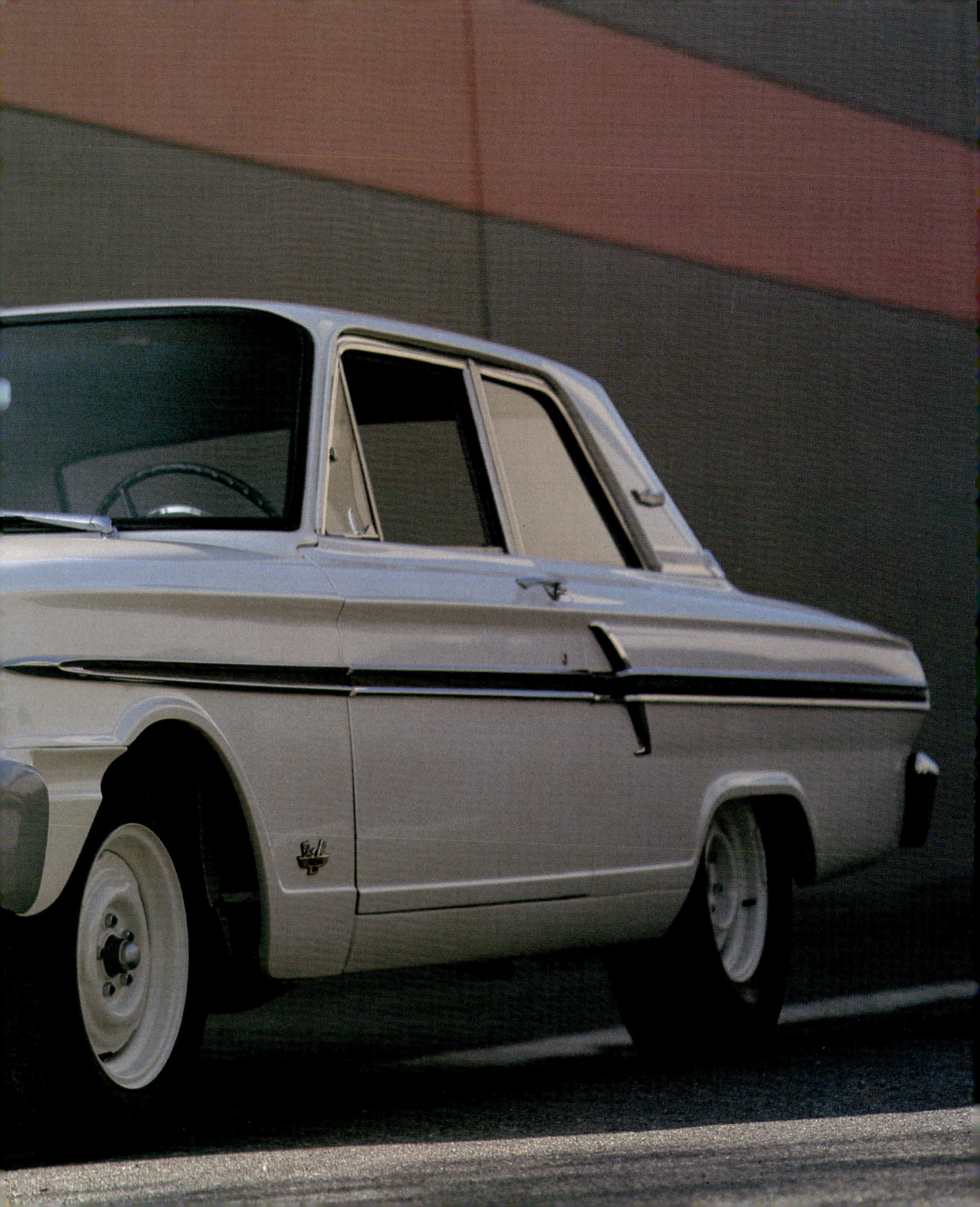

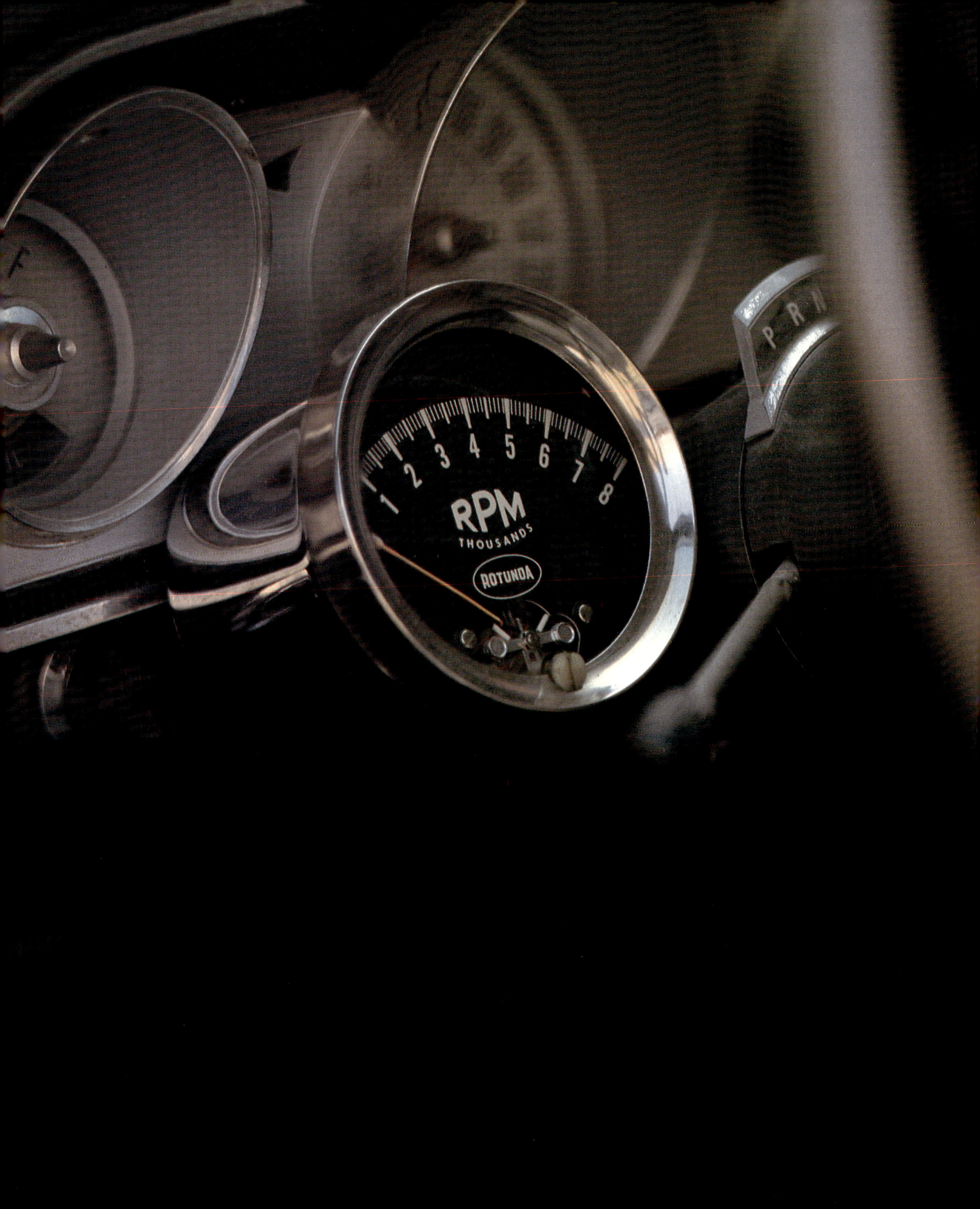
1 2 3 4 5 6 7 8
RPM
THOUSANDS
ROTUNDA
P R N

The interior of the Thunderbolt was Spartan, with the stock bench seat replaced by two Econoline van buckets. Also removed were radio, heater, armrests, rear-view mirror, as well as sound insulation. The windshield was stock, but the side and rear panes were replaced by plexiglass reproductions. Special metal tabs were attached to the outside of the rear window frame to help hold the window in place. A Rotunda tachometer—featured here—further indicated the serious nature of the vehicle. The automatic transmission used in the original Thunderbolt was a modified Lincoln unit. A few cars came equipped with four-speed manuals, and these turned out to be somewhat faster. The Lincoln transmission proved to be troublesome, and most Thunderbolts had them replaced by Borg-Warner units.

*A*s installed in the 1964 Thunderbolt, Ford's 427 represents a peak of the period. This legend among racing engines featured high-riser-type heads with machined combustion chambers, forged steel crankshaft and pop-up-type pistons. The compression ratio was a tight 12.7:1. Dual four-barrel Holleys were placed above a special aluminum intake manifold. Topping off this maze of metal was a cast-aluminum induction box, to the right, which channeled fresh air to the carburetor through flexible ducts connected to the screened, hollowed-out headlight bezels, pictured above. Ford claimed an output of 425 horses. But the actual figure was thought to be more like 500—a belief reflected by NHRA's own refactoring figures.

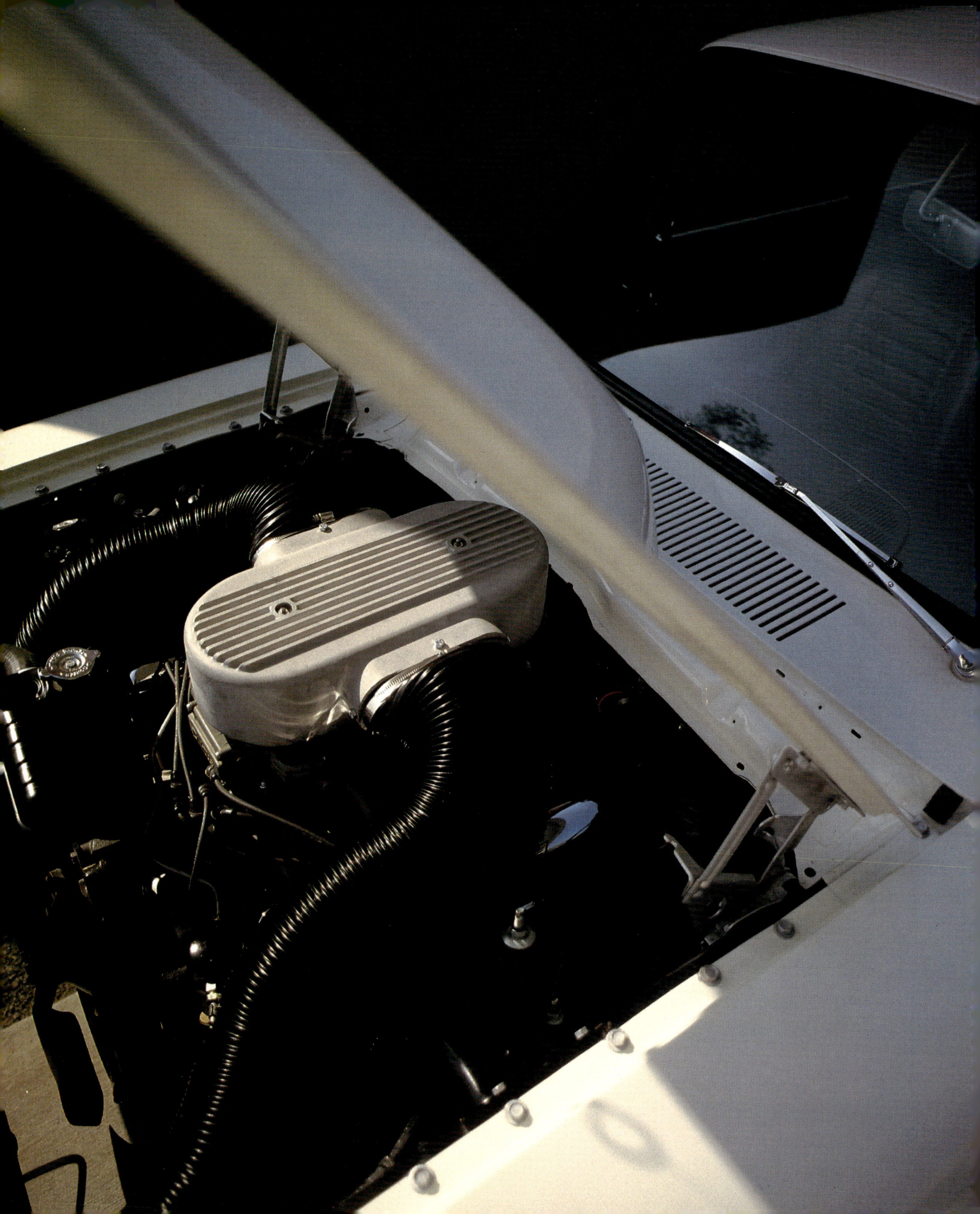

1964 Pontiac LeMans GTO

Muscle for the masses

*B*urnout at the GTO corral.

Late in 1963, readers of the December issue of Hot Rod magazine were aroused by a clever attention-grabbing ad. Below a group of photos featuring such intriguing objects as a Hurst shifter, a pair of gleaming exhaust splitters and a Rochester carburetor, a subtle headline whispered this tantalizing message: "For the man who wouldn't mind riding a tiger if someone'd only put wheels on it—Pontiac GTO."

It was no coincidence that advertising played a vital role in the making of the GTO image. One of the driving forces behind this trendsetter of a machine was Jim Wangers, an account executive at Pontiac's advertising agency. But before the GTO became depicted in printer's ink, the concept had been developed on the drawing board—an accomplishment attributed to John DeLorean, then Pontiac's chief engineer.

DeLorean had arrived at Pontiac in 1956. After generating such soul-stirring items as the Tri-Power 389 and the early Super-Duty 389, the flamboyant engineer was promoted to his kingpin post in 1961. Then, in 1963, came the corporate ban on racing. The decree not only put an end to involvement on the track, it also limited the size of standard engines that could be placed in General Motors' small and medium-size cars.

But DeLorean could not be stopped. As worded, the ban could be construed as applying only to "standard" engines. Thus the GTO, with its big 389 under the hood, was introduced as an option in the LeMans series. It was a move destined to become hotly debated in the corporate corridors. In the end, no one was willing to argue with success—the GTO sold to the tune of 32,000 units that first year.

The concept of combining a big engine with a medium-size body—the principle that created the muscle car—had been tried before. But the mass marketing potential of such a combination was not realized until DeLorean invented the GTO—today affectionately called the Goat.

The 1964 model was only the beginning. For 1965, the body design was revised. The GTO now sported stacked headlights, which made it longer and increased the weight by 340 pounds. Sales were also up, soaring as high as 75,000.

For 1966, the GTO was moved away from the LeMans line and became a model on its own. Although the exterior alterations left the basic look intact, there were a number of detail changes, among them a revised grille and three-slitted taillights. A record number of nearly 97,000 units were sold.

The 1967 model marked the end of the first generation. The grille was changed again to feature the popular egg-crate look. Also changed were the rocker panels—which became wider—and, once more, the taillights—which became four separate units. Sales were down slightly, to about 82,000 units.

The 1964 GTO not only marked the official launch of the muscle car, it also placed the career of its chief instigator into a rising orbit—DeLorean was made general manager of Pontiac in 1965. From this position, he went on to father new generations of famous Pontiacs—among them, the 1967 Firebird and the 1968 GTO.

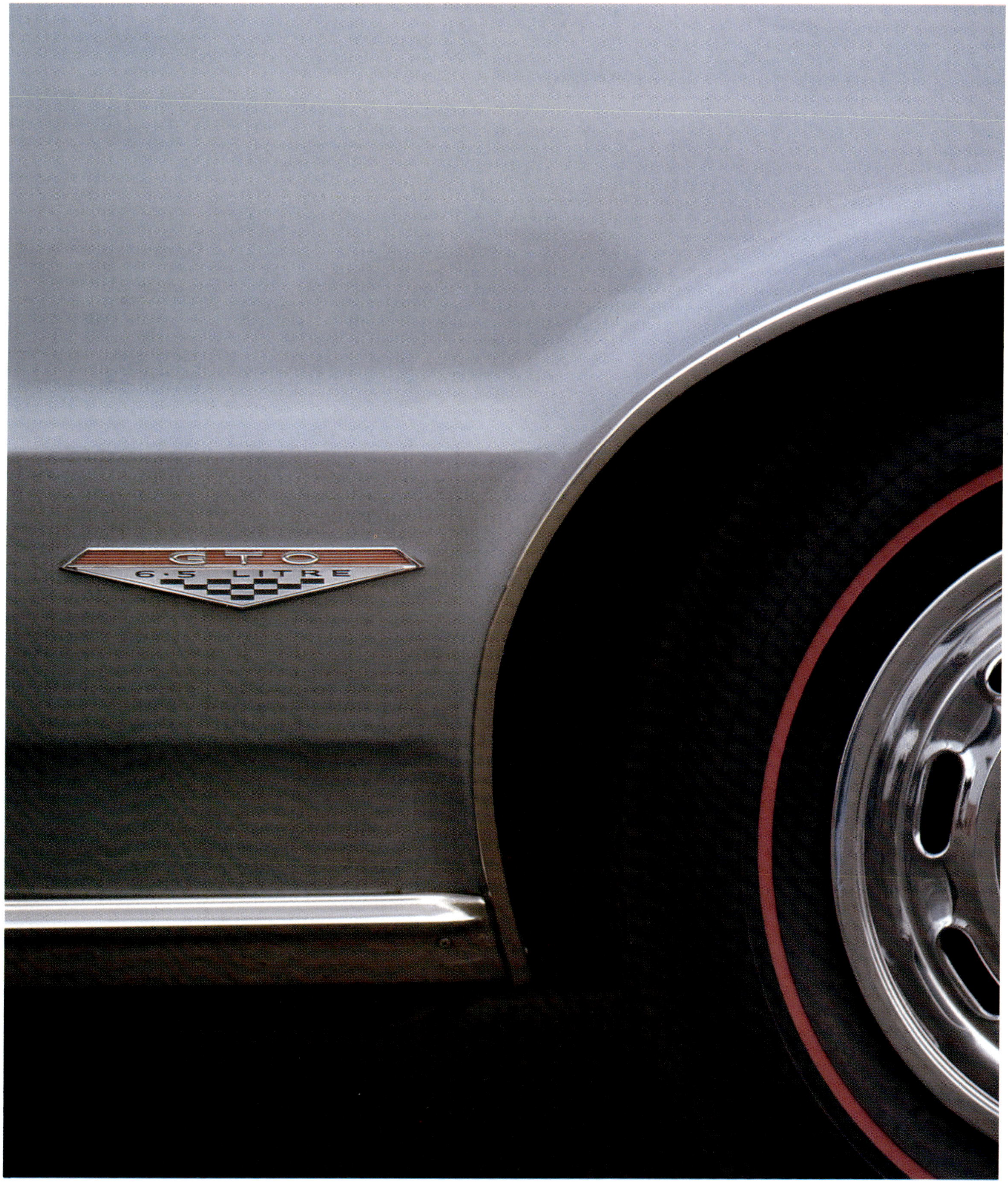
GTO
6.5 LITRE

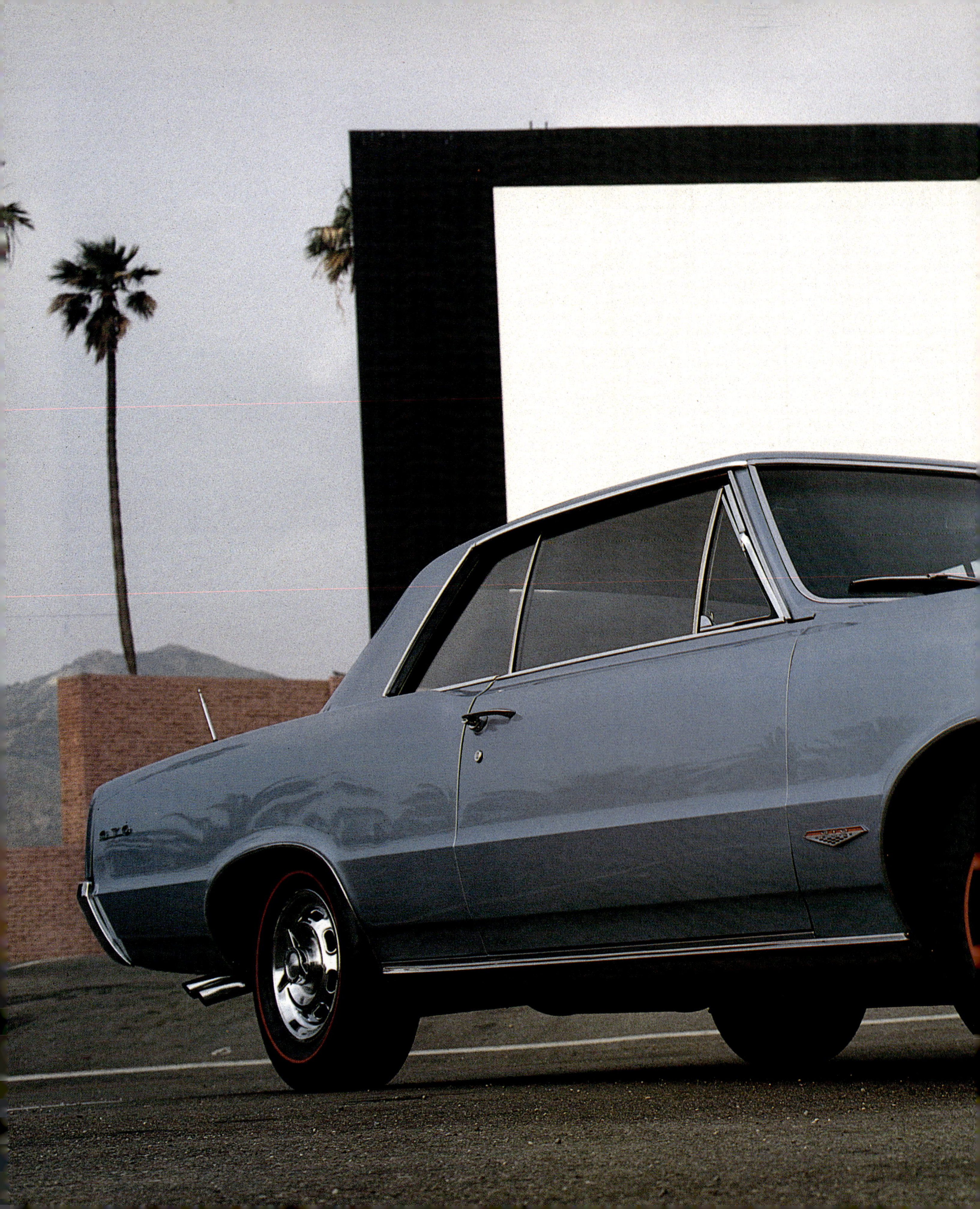

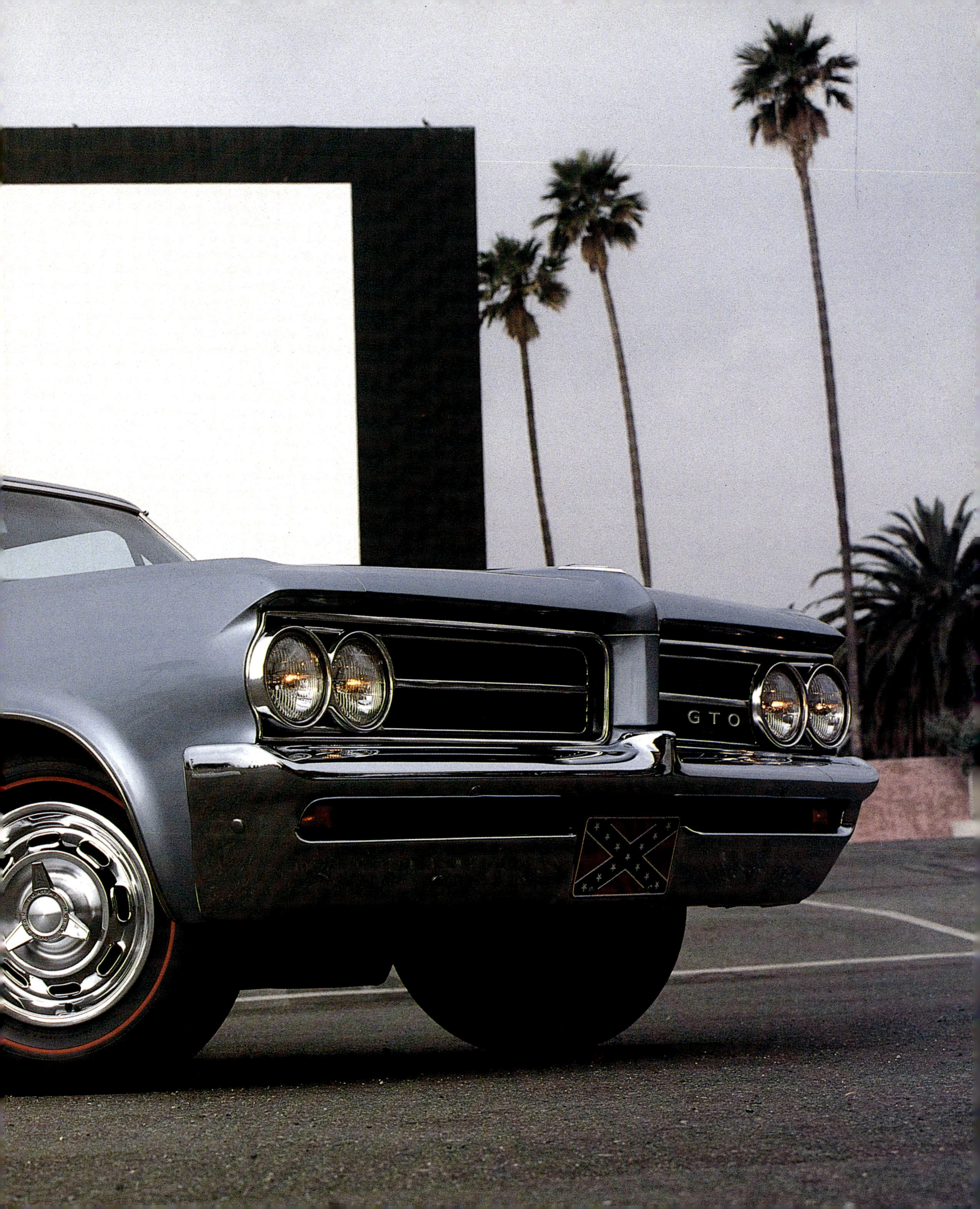
GTO

In 1964, the exterior of the GTO was nothing more than a cleverly made-over Tempest. In an attempt to create a more aggressive look, the grille had been blacked-out. Also adding to the visual excitement was the liberal use of the GTO badge—complete with a checkered-flag pattern. It appeared both on the side panels—as seen on the opening pages of this chapter—as well as on the rear deck lid. Also added for appearance only were the two hood scoops—they were not yet functional.

Other changes, however, were not cosmetic—the GTO chassis sported stiffer springs, special shock absorbers and quicker steering. Body styles were coupe, hardtop and convertible. The hardtop—priced at $2,786—was most common, totaling 18,442 units of the 32,450 built. The coupe was duplicated 7,384 times. Rarest is the convertible, re-created in 6,644 copies. The 1964 version of the GTO is without question the most historically significant of the four models included in the first generation.

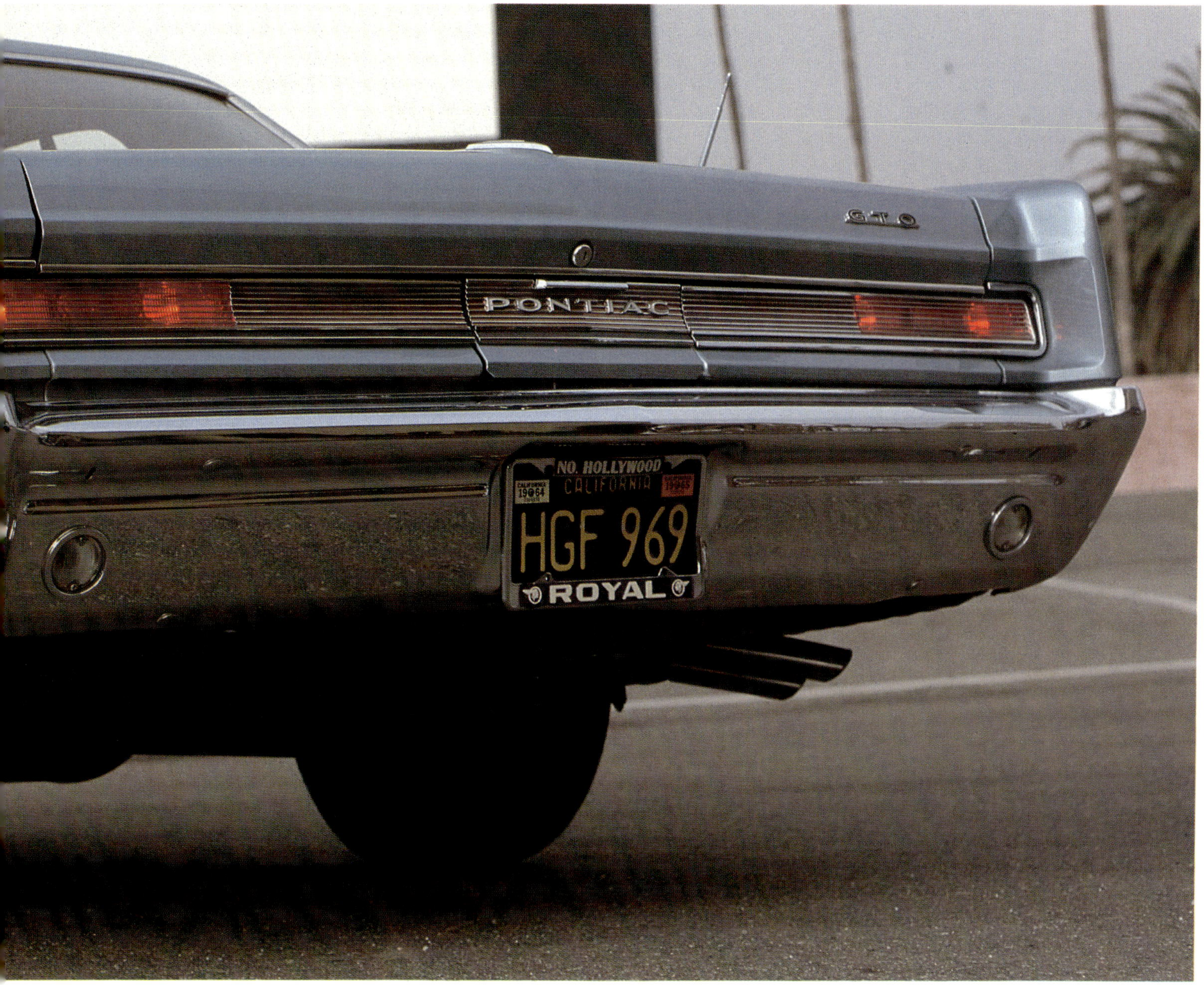
GTO
PONTIAC
NO. HOLLYWOOD
CALIFORNIA
HGF 969
ROYAL

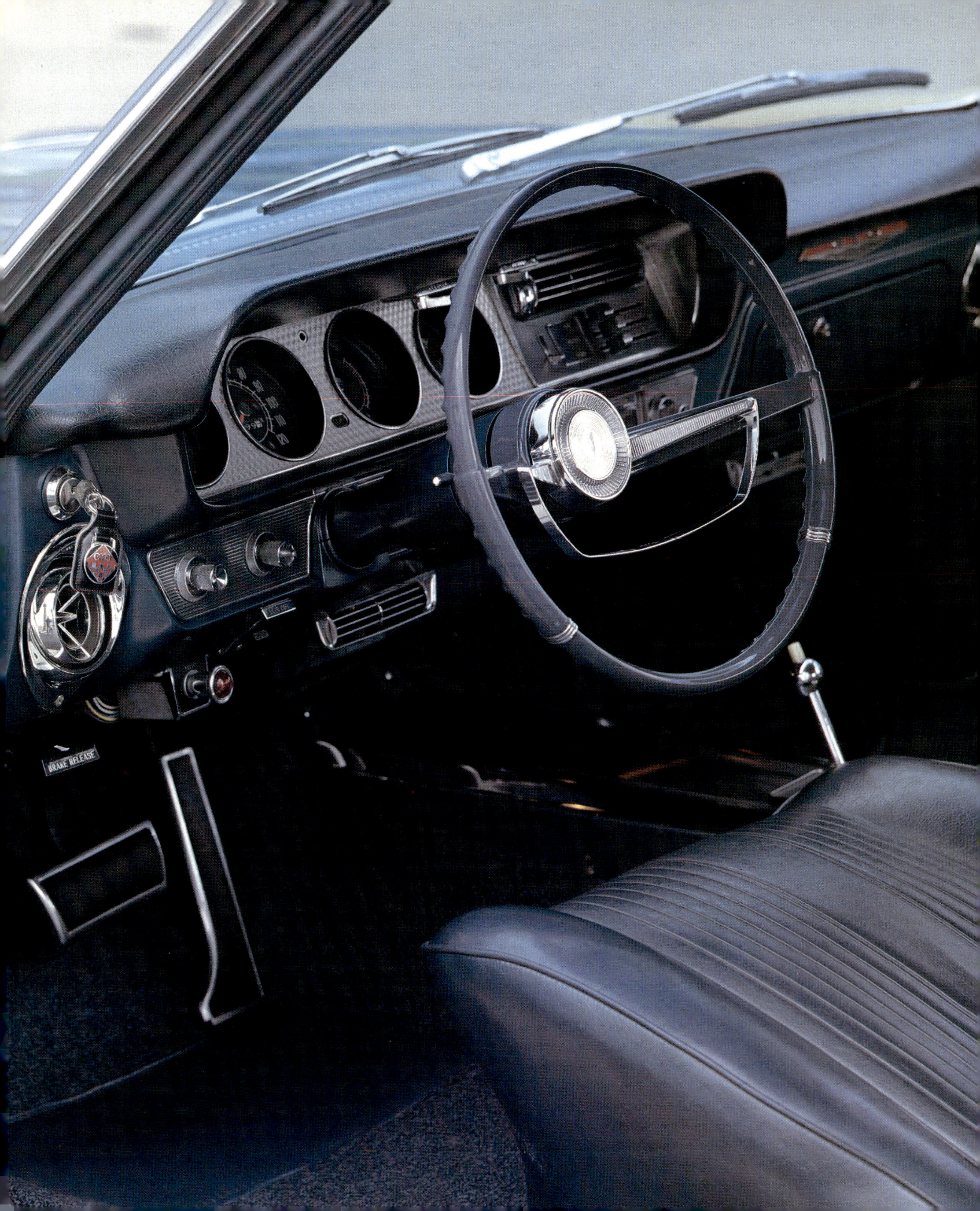
BRAKE RELEASE

*T*he interior of the original GTO was only moderately sporty in its standard configuration, to the left, although it did feature bucket seats in place of the conventional bench. For added sportiness one could order an optional Sports steering wheel, which featured four thin spokes, and an optional tachometer, which was placed in the right-most instrument pod. A three-speed transmission, actuated via a white-knobbed stick on the floor, was standard fare. Other transmission options included an all-synchromesh four-speed on the floor, an automatic unit operated via a column-mounted lever, or—as pictured above—a lever located in a console between the seats. Exterior colors were carefully coordinated. This car, which was one of the first to come off the line—completed the second week of December 1963—contrasts a Nocturne Blue interior with a Yorktown Blue exterior.

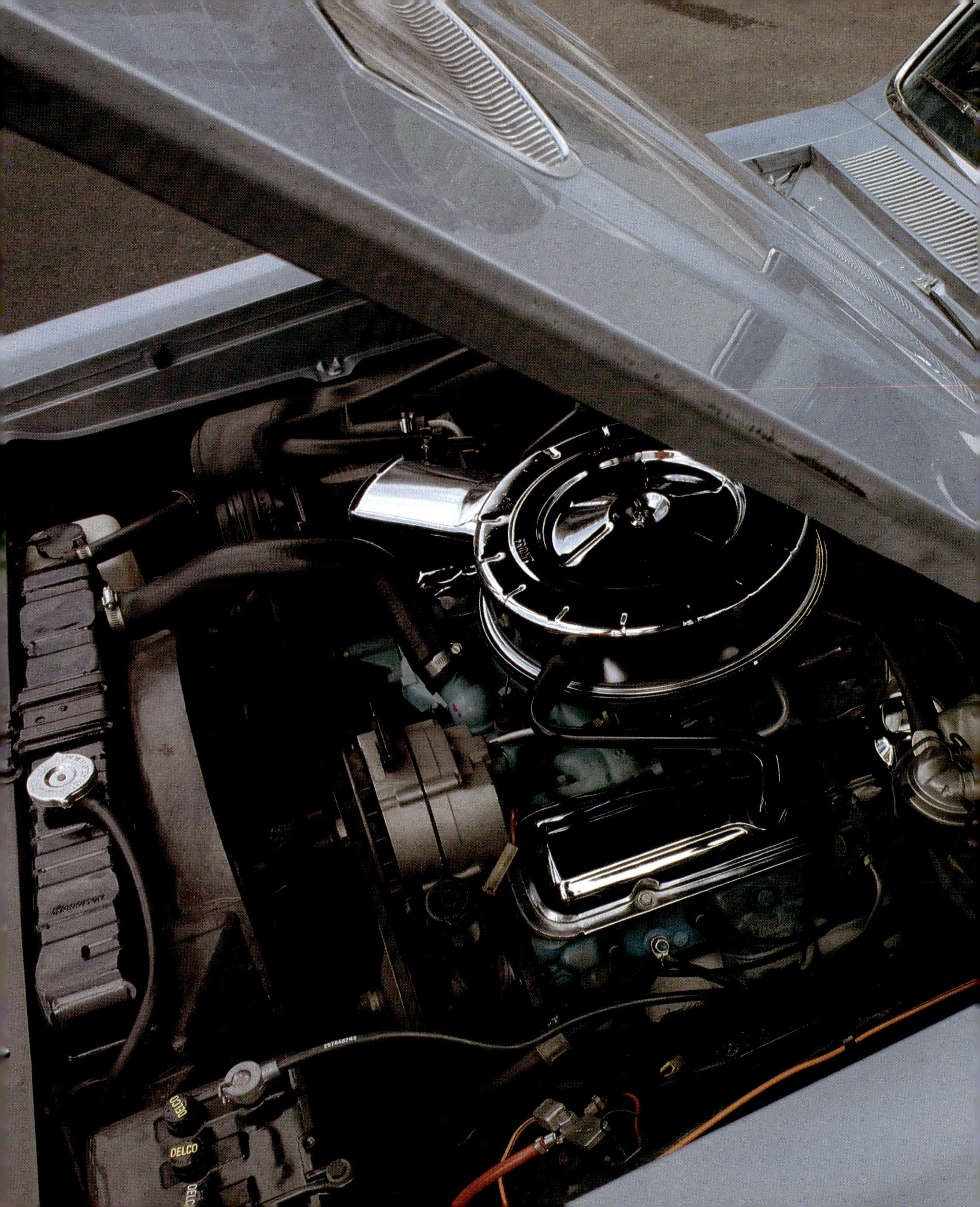
DELCO

The exterior manifestations of power found on the GTO, such as hood scoops, checkered-flag badges and dual exhaust pipes, were justified in the sense that they complemented the honest power packed into the engine compartment. In standard configuration—shown here—the 389 ci unit produced as much as 325 hp at 4800 rpm. This was achieved through a number of measures—a special cylinder head increased compression to 10.75:1, and special high-rate valve springs worked with high-performance camshafts. Breathing was facilitated by a single four-barrel Carter, topped by a chromed snorkel-type air cleaner. The Tri-Power option employed three twin-barrel Rochesters to squeeze out another 23 horses. Of the total production, 8,245 were equipped with this option. Acceleration was truly spectacular—the 0-60 mph time took just 4.6 seconds. On the drag strip, the Tri-Power, when fitted with slicks, would blow the shirt off the back of the competition with quarter-mile times in the high twelves. No wonder the GTO won an instant following among performance buffs.

1966 Plymouth Satellite 426 Hemi

The Hemi hits the street

Plain-Jane never moved faster.

Performance enthusiasts have always been intrigued by machines that look like plain-Jane automobiles but move like fiery Atlas rockets. In the early seventies, even a conservative manufacturer like Mercedes-Benz fell for the temptation to play the game, mating its potent 6.3 liter V-8 to its top-of-the-line sedan. The result was the 300SEL, a machine that fooled fellow motorists with its blistering performance.

Five years earlier, in 1966, the same philosophy had produced an American example of this type of car—the Plymouth Satellite 426 Hemi. And, although the Mopar product had a five-year technology handicap and weighed 520 pounds more, the Detroit machine would have run a dead race with the Mercedes. The Plymouth Satellite was indeed the ultimate plain-Jane. And its secret lay in the formidable Hemi engine.

Chrysler Corporation was certainly familiar with the Hemi concept. It had introduced its first version in 1951. At that time the 355 ci motor put out 180 hp. Later, as fitted to the 1955 Chrysler 300, the unit produced 300 horses and went on to dominate the sands of Daytona. But by 1958, at a time when the Hemi had been bored out to its maximum 392 ci, the trend toward bigger engines, combined with the high production cost of the complex Chrysler design—which translated into a high price in the showroom—killed off the original Hemi.

Then, in 1963, it was time to dust off the old design and return to the drawing board. Powered by the 426 Wedge motor, Plymouth—now the purveyor of the Mopar competition tradition—was totally outclassed on the NASCAR circuit. At the 1963 Daytona, for example, Richard Petty—the fastest of the Plymouth pilots—managed only a distant sixth. The first five spots belonged to Ford and its Total Performance 427.

By the following season's Daytona, however, the Plymouths were powered by the redesigned Hemi, and the tables were turned—the Mopar team, led by Petty, took the first three places. The Hemi went on to such an overwhelming NASCAR season that the governing body decided to outlaw it. The reason given was that the Hemi did not conform to the formula of a stock engine—in other words, it was not available in a street machine. Thus, during the 1965 season, the Mopar team was put out of the competition, a fact not to be tolerated. The remedy came in the form of the plain-Jane Plymouth Satellite 426 Hemi.

During the production period of the Hemi motors, which lasted from 1964 to 1971, approximately 10,000 units were built. About 800 ended up in Satellites, a model that turned out to be a one-year phenomenon, since it was replaced by the GTX the following year.

Since most of the Hemi motors used to power the Satellites were ultimately transferred to all-out racing machines, there are extremely few stock Satellites still around. The example featured here, a citron-gold beauty, is totally original and unrestored. The present owner bought the survivor in 1969 with 14,000 miles on the odometer.

The Satellite Hemi is indeed a rare machine—and one of the definitive milestones along the muscle car road.

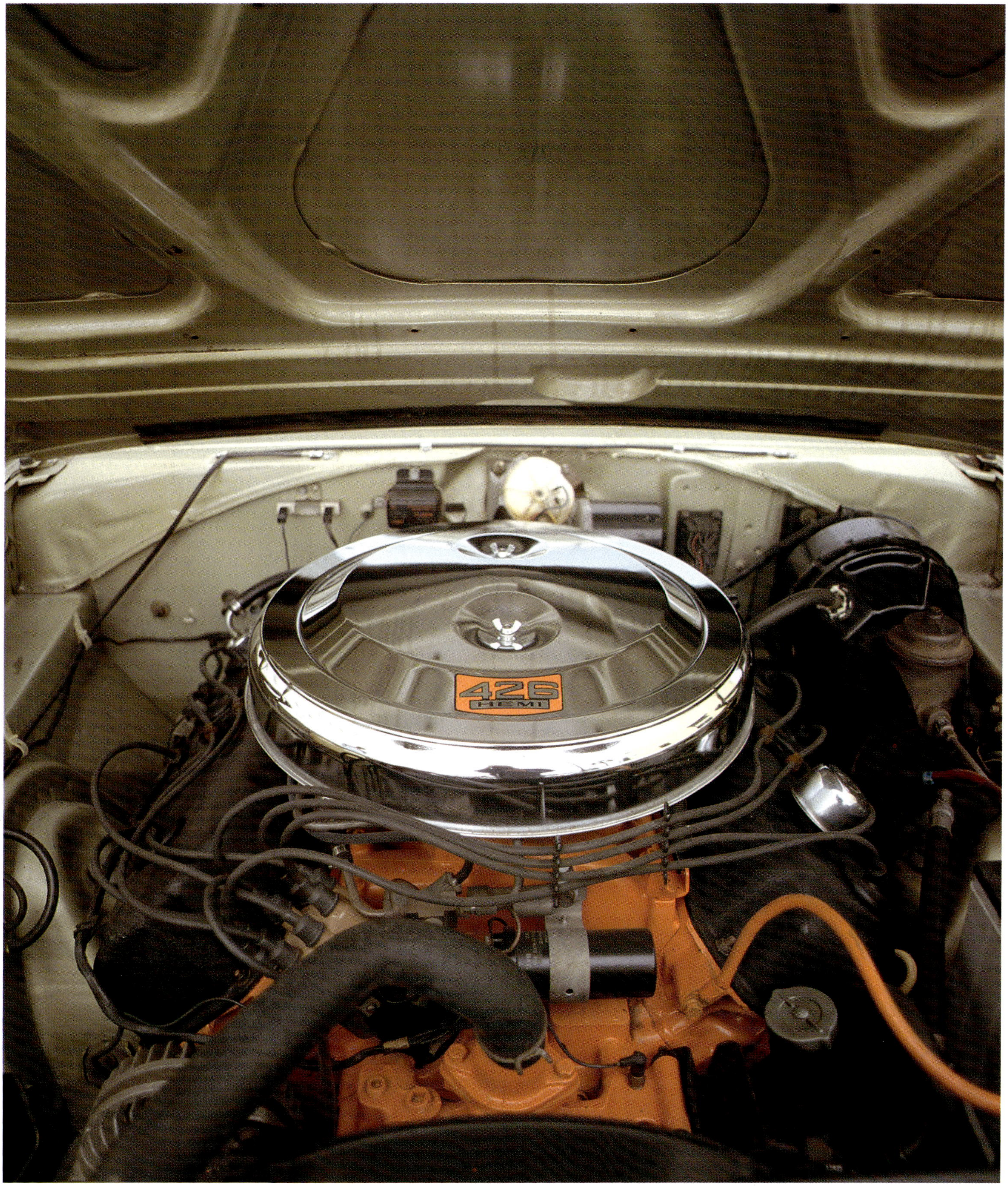
426
HEMI

The picture on the previous page shows a wide-angle view of the formidable power package hidden beneath the sedate exterior of the Plymouth Satellite 426 Hemi. While producing as much as 650 hp with the patented cross-ram system used for racing, the Hemi for the street generated "only" 425 hp at 5200 rpm. Compression was 10.25:1. Breathing was administered through two four-barrel Carter carburetors. Zero-to-sixty mph took just over seven seconds. The quarter-mile was covered in 14.5 seconds. The basic Satellite, which was powered by Chrysler's 273 ci unit, carried a price tag of $2,695. Opting for the Hemi meant a further $1,105, which is why the car was most often purchased by drivers with a serious intent. Who else would pay such a hefty penalty for a car that looked as though it were built for the driveway of a retired FBI agent? The side view pictured here, and the following rear view certainly do not transmit vibrations of spine-tingling excitement. But, as is often the case, looks are deceiving. For the performance buff, the Satellite provided a docile drive to the drag strip, but once out on that quarter-mile stretch of rubber-streaked asphalt, it became a ferocious machine, fit to tangle with the fastest.

59

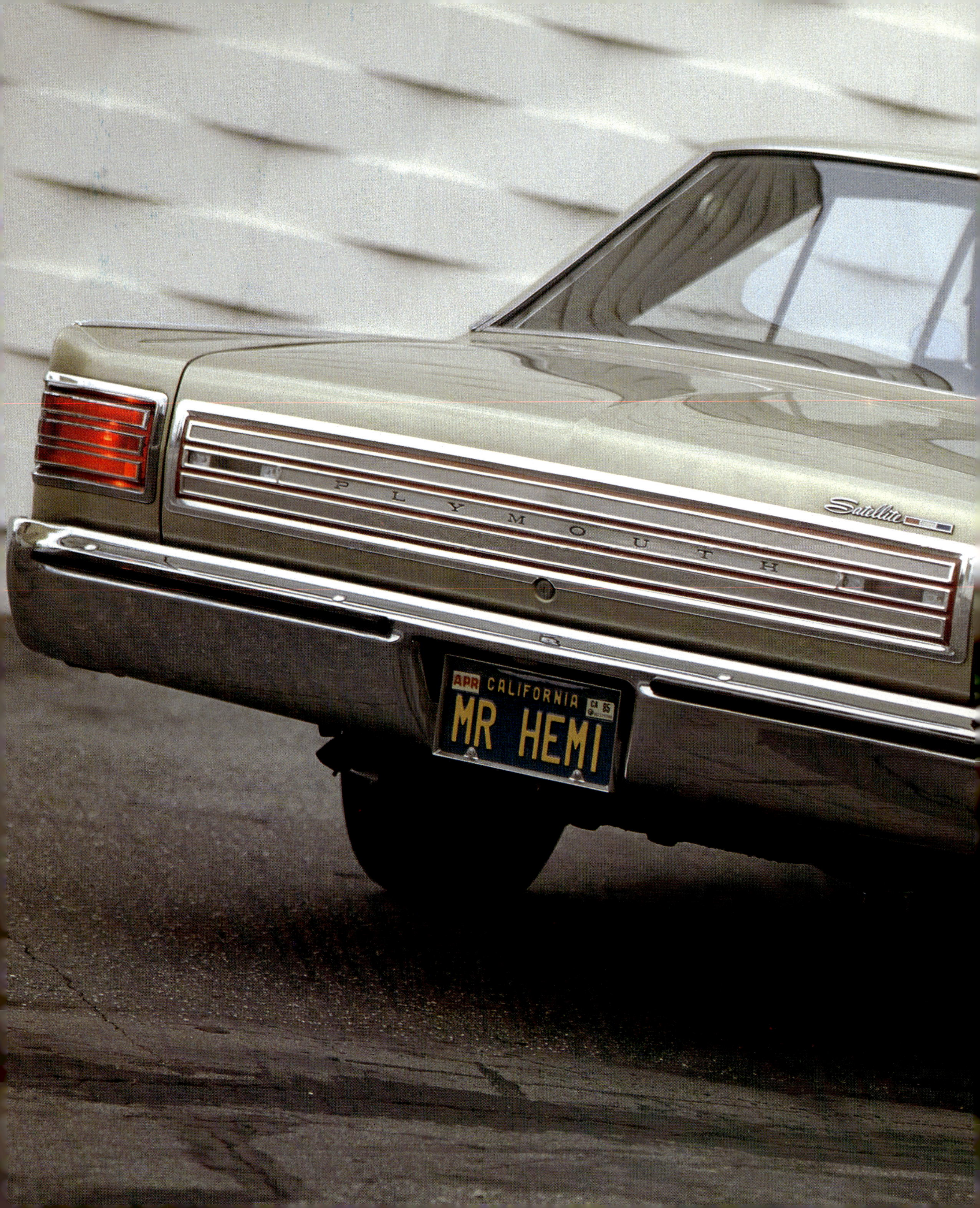
PLYMOUTH
Satellite
APR CALIFORNIA
MR HEMI

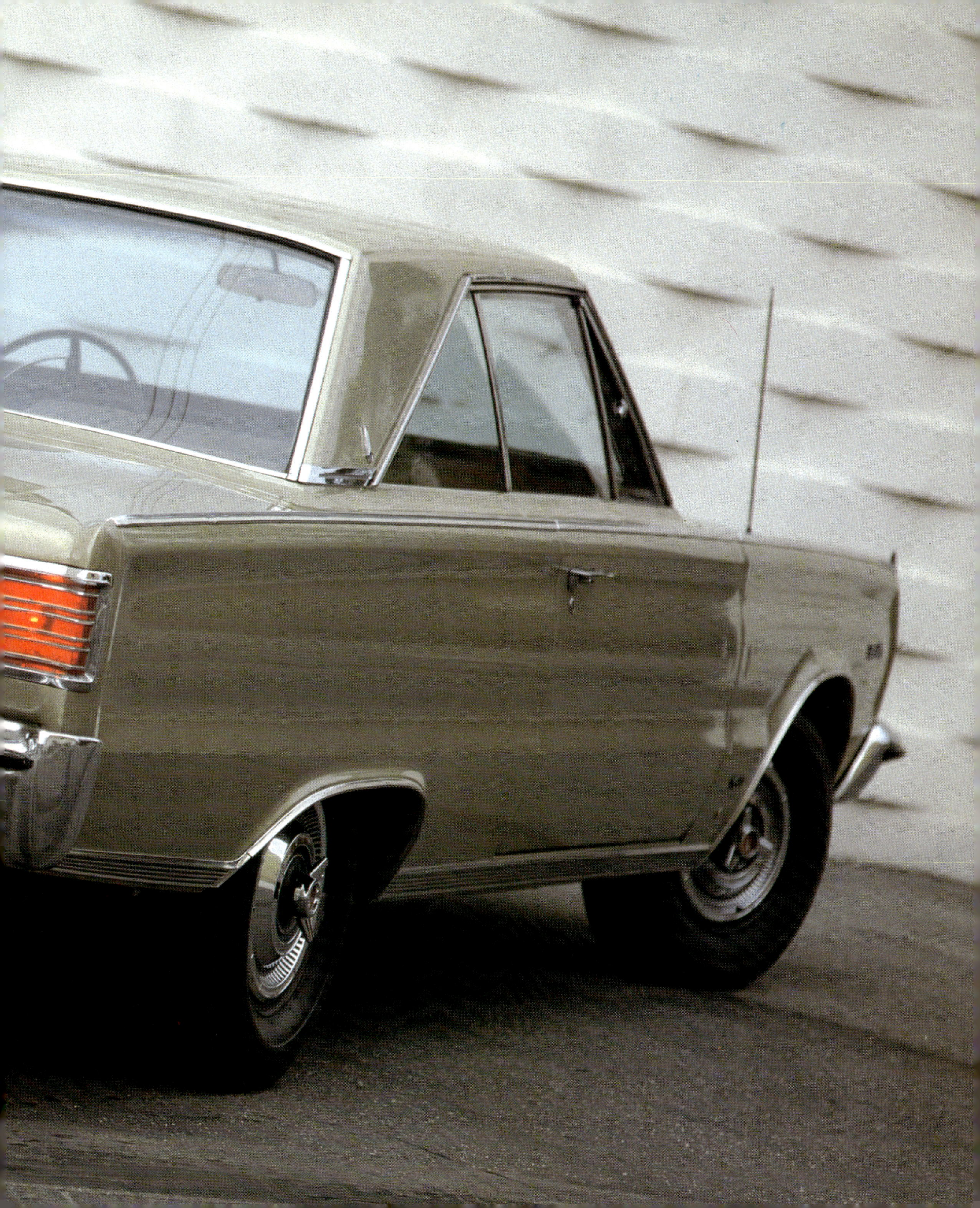

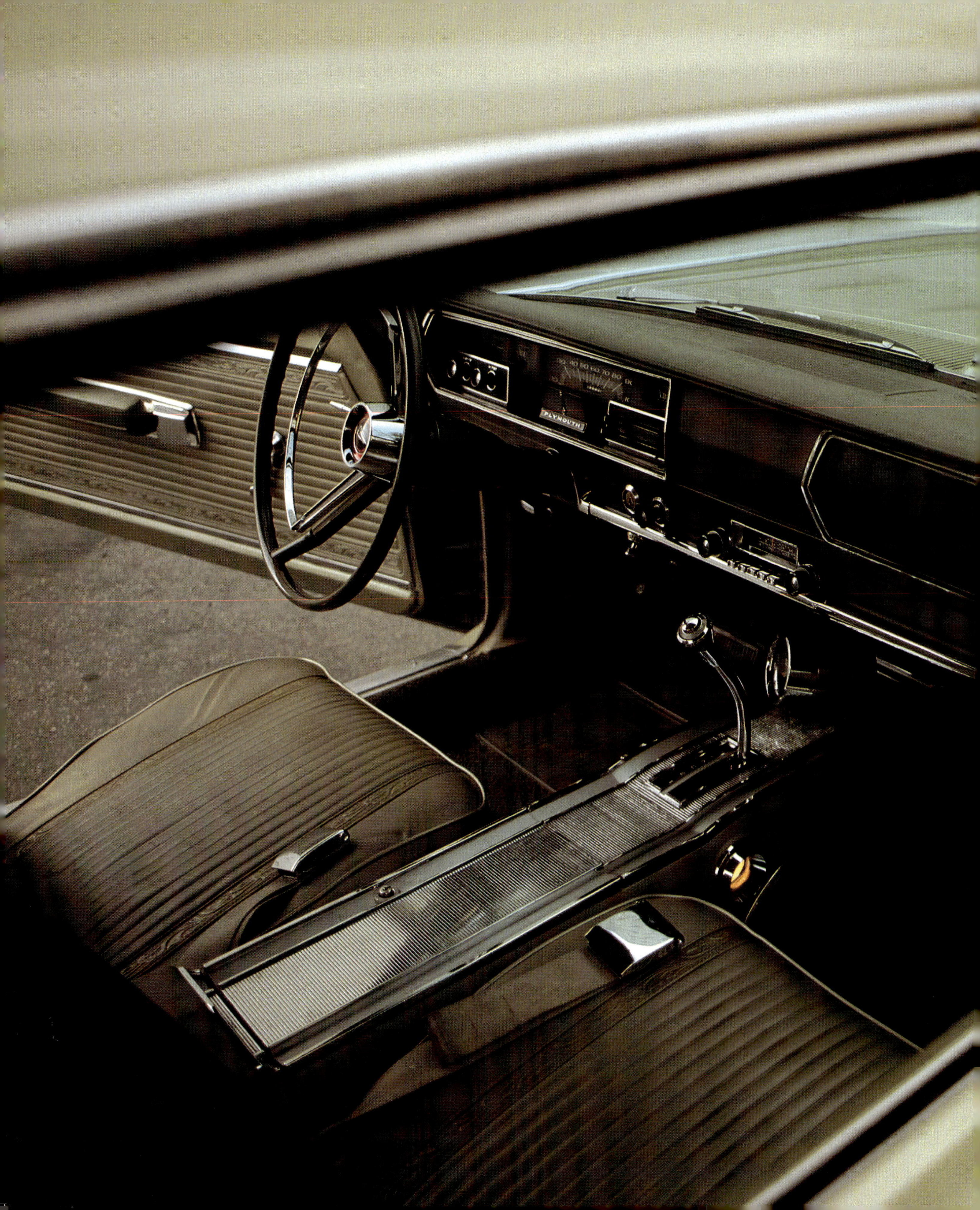
PLYMOUTH

If the exterior of the Plymouth Satellite 426 Hemi possessed an aura of mild-mannered family car, the interior certainly followed suit. The only item indicating that there might be something unusual hiding under the hood was the tachometer. This option—priced at $48.35—was the target of some negative comments by the contemporary reviewers. Its awkward location on the console required "a long swing for the eyes while executing all-out acceleration runs, during which full use of the tachometer is mandatory." The shift lever, also mounted on the console, was mated to a three-speed automatic—Chrysler's heavy-duty TorqueFlite. A four-speed manual transmission was also available. In a road test performed by Car Life magazine, the TorqueFlite was found to shift from first to second at 4900 rpm and from second to third at 5200 rpm.

1967 Pontiac Firebird 400 HO

First of the fire-breathers

First Firebird—a 1954 gas turbine car.

Ford's 1964 introduction of the Mustang injected a brand new breed into the American automotive scene. It was a formula inspired by the two-plus-two concept popularized by European grand touring machines. But while rear-seat accommodation in overseas counterparts was limited, usually for children, Detroit's two-plus-two machines—conforming to the inherently larger scale of American cars—were spacious enough to provide room for four full-grown individuals.

This was the birth of the pony car concept. And it proved to be a stroke of genius on the part of Ford. More than 120,000 Mustangs were sold the first year. The next year, sales exploded to an incredible 560,000 units. Other American auto makers were caught by surprise, and began a scramble to conceive pony cars of their own.

It took less than the customary three-year period for the gestation of a new model before General Motors brought out an answer to the Mustang. The response was two-pronged, with Chevrolet's Camaro and Pontiac's Firebird sharing the basic body style. Chrysler Corporation was slower in reacting to the new trend, and did not have a true pony car until 1970—almost too late—when the Dodge Challenger and the second-generation Plymouth Barracuda were introduced.

The first Firebird emerged from the Lordstown, Ohio, plant in early January. Pontiac executives were moderately optimistic about the success of the new model, and made plans for a 50,000 production run. As it turned out, sales were much better than expected, and totaled 82,560 units for 1967.

The Firebird was available in two body configurations, coupe and convertible, and came with three basic engine options. At the bottom of the ladder was the Sprint, powered by a 215 hp overhead-cam six. A three-speed manual transmission with floor-mounted stick was standard. A price tag of $2,782 for the coupe made the basic Firebird quite affordable, although a Mustang equipped with a 200 hp V-8 cost $215 less.

The next step up the ladder was occupied by a 326 V-8, producing 250 hp, and breathing through a twin-barrel carburetor. The 326 HO, high output, represented another step up, and had a 285 hp V-8 under the hood. The additional power was extracted through increased compression and the use of a four-barrel carburetor. A three-speed manual transmission with column-mounted shift lever was standard. Added performance also added to the price—the coupe cost $2,825.

At the top of the ladder was the 400 and its HO option. Power came from a 400 ci V-8. Output was 335 hp at 5000 rpm. A total of 6,078 units were made. An optional Ram Air system—available for an additional $600—drew air through functional hood scoops, and used higher output cams and valve springs to raise the peak of the power curve. Just 100 units were built of this optimal fire-breather.

Pontiac's Firebird went on to greater things in 1969, with the new Trans Am. But the 1967 original will always occupy a special niche among Firebird enthusiasts.

65

The Firebird shared its basic body with corporate cousin Camaro. But the Pontiac stylists managed to stamp their own mark on the design. Most distinctive was the treatment of the front end, where the divided grille lent a more aggressive expression—as in the photograph on the following page. The pointed nose, in turn, added length and grace to the hood—as in this picture. Actually, just 4.3 inches had been added. But the Firebird also weighed 225 pounds more than its Camaro counterpart, taking its toll in the performance department. Pictured on the previous page, the view under the hood of the 400. The HO version was certainly no slouch—0-60 mph took just 5.5 seconds. The quarter-mile was covered in 14.2 seconds.

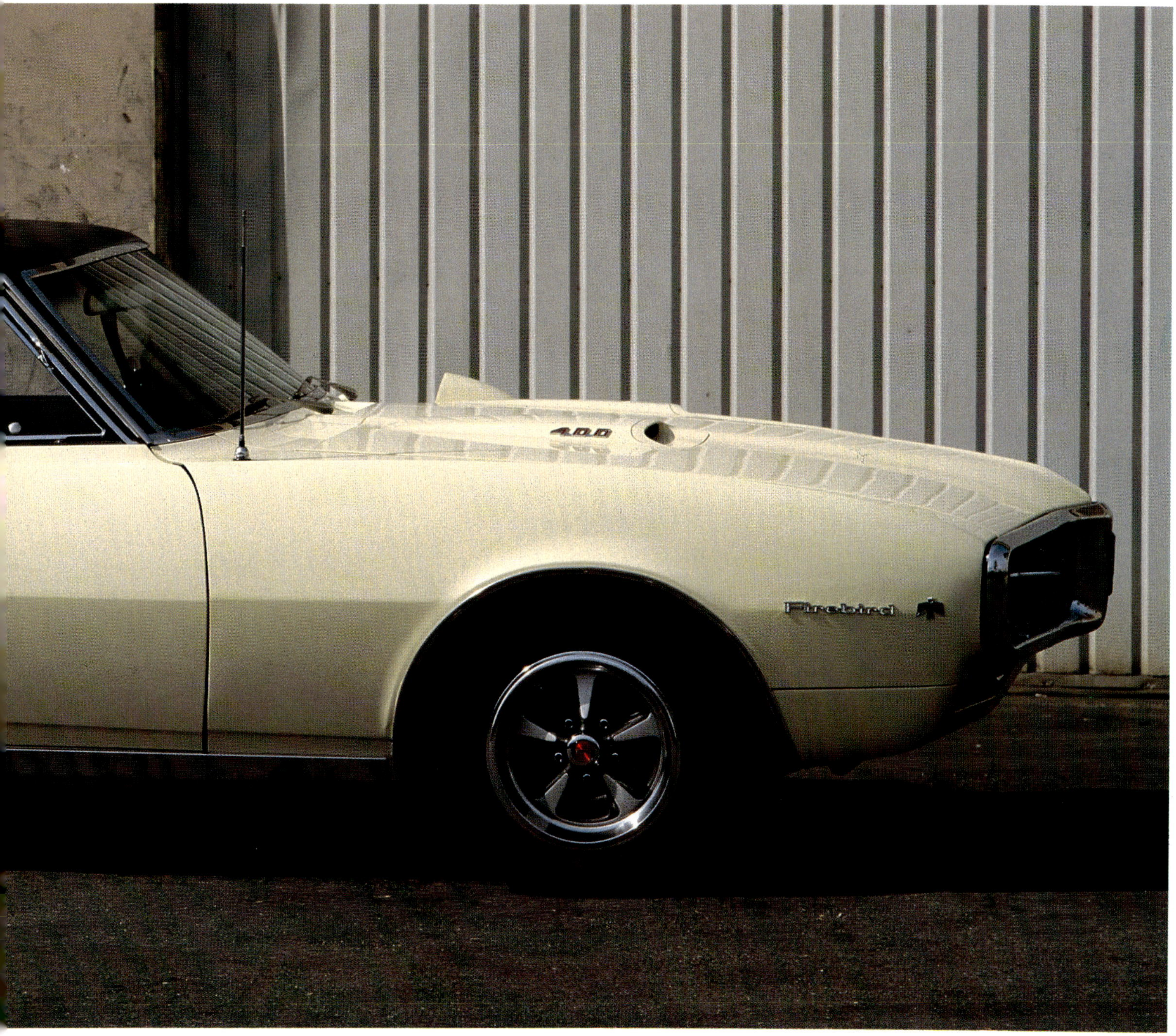
400
Firebird

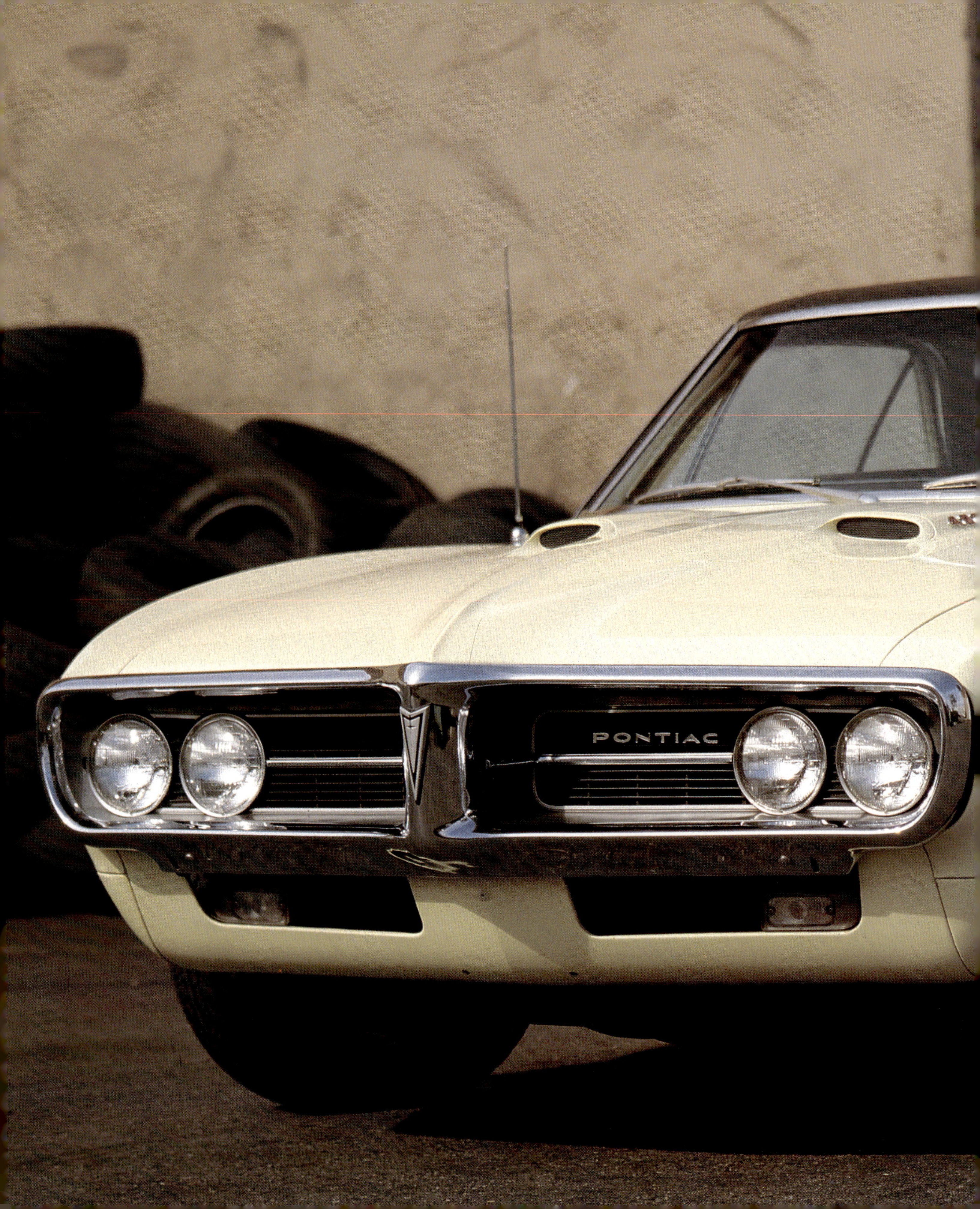
PONTIAC

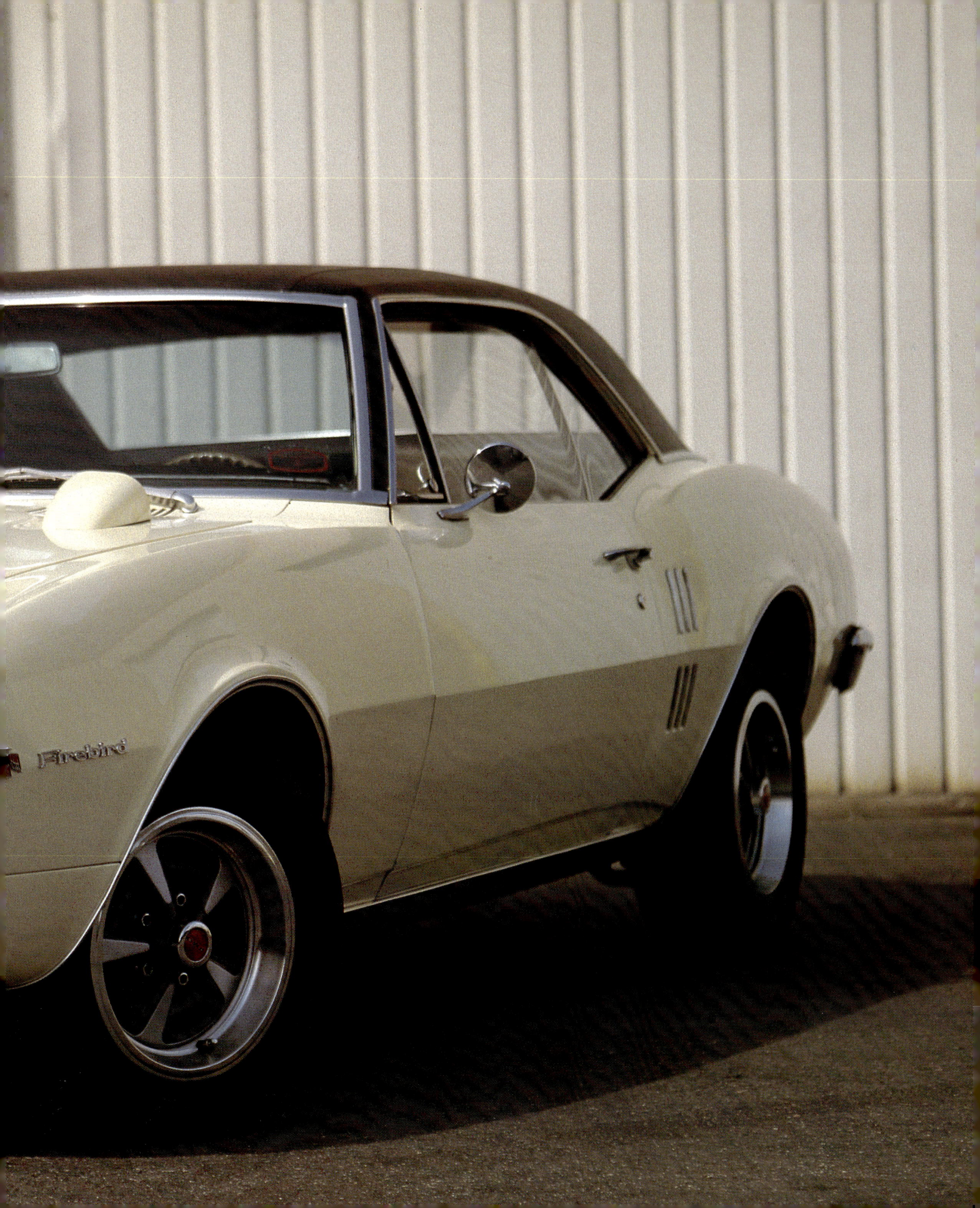
Firebird

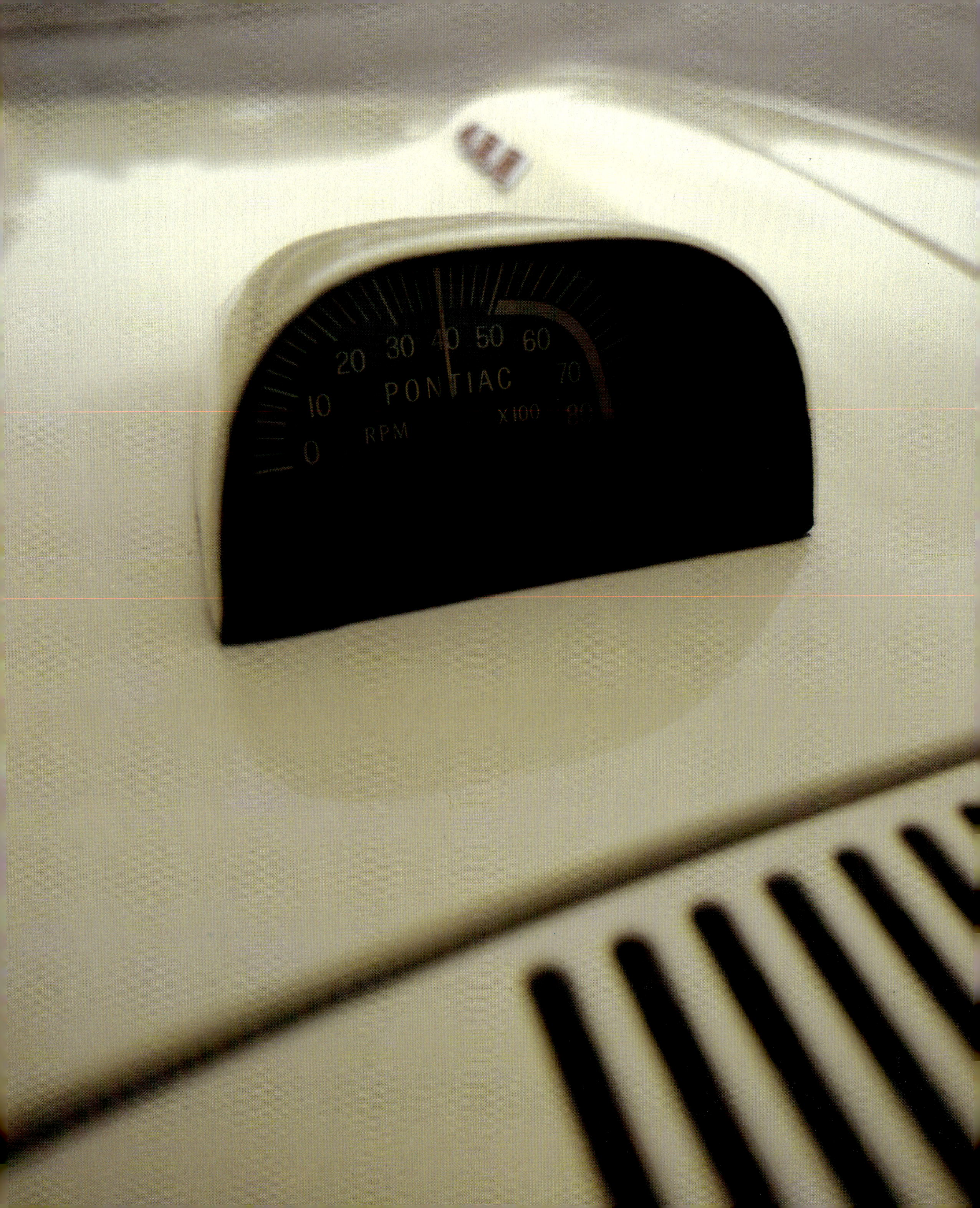
0
10
20
30
40
50
60
70
80
PONTIAC
RPM
X100

Much of the image of the muscle car was just that—image. This stemmed as much from the application of superficial elements as from real and honest features. Two of the favorite image builders of the era are pictured here. To the left, the exterior tachometer, which—most of the time—was not such a bad idea. The location out on the hood actually placed it right in the driver's line of vision. On the negative side, however, the instrument often had to endure a most hostile environment, and, if nothing worse happened, it tended to fog up at the most inopportune times. Coupled to the rheostat of the dashboard-mounted gauges, the hood tach lit up with the application of the headlights, which made a most intriguing sight during nocturnal excursions. The splitters, pictured above, were certainly functional as well, but the doubling-up of the pipes and their posed placement were purely for effect. Mission accomplished.

1969 Camaro Baldwin Motion Phase III

Emergence of a moth-balled missile

Cornering a la Camaro.

Chevrolet introduced its first-born pony car, the Camaro, on September 29, 1966, thus beating corporate neighbor Pontiac—with whom it shared the body style—by nearly five months.

In spite of this lead, sales figures for the inaugural year were surprisingly low—just under 100,000 units, which was not that much more than first-year sales of the Firebird. But the following year saw a tremendous upswing, as the Camaro lengthened its stride—235,000 units took to the road.

The original pony car, Ford's Mustang, was still going strong at 317,000 units for 1968, but the bite was beginning to weaken, as indicated by the fact that total sales dropped below the 300,000 mark in 1969, a year when the Camaro introduced new styling and again hit the 230,000 figure.

Part of the Camaro's success can be attributed to the fact that, in addition to the reasonably low base price, there was such a tremendous variety of options available to meet a broad spectrum of tastes and needs. The base Camaro came in two body configurations, coupe and convertible, costing $2,466 and $2,704 respectively.

The base engine was an inline six, producing 140 hp at 4400 rpm. It was coupled to a three-speed manual transmission. The next step up placed a V-8 under the hood. This unit was a 327 ci version, producing 210 hp. Further options scaled the performance ladder, with a 302 ci, 290 hp unit; a 350 ci, 295 hp; a 396 ci, 325 hp; and finally, the 396 ci tweaked to 375 hp—the famous L-28 option.

The 1969 styling change introduced new excitement to the Camaro, and resulted in a longer and lower look. The body sides were now more sculptured, with a sharp crease flowing rearward from the upper edges of each of the wheelwells. A Super Scoop added further visual excitement to the Super Sport and the Z-28 option packages.

There were some rare, little-known Camaros issued for 1969, such as the Indianapolis Pace Car replica, of which fifty copies were built and distributed to race dignitaries. There are also records supporting the contention that another 3,629 units were assembled for sale to the public.

The most fascinating among the limited-edition Camaros was the ZL-1, a machine powered by Chevrolet's ferocious aluminum-block 427, putting out as much as 425 hp. The ZL-1 Camaros were produced for factory racing, and a total of sixty-nine units were made—slightly more than the fifty-car limit required by the homologation rules.

The fascination with the Camaro among the performance set was such that more elaborate power concoctions began to flourish. These were initiated by Chevrolet dealers, and included names such as Don Nickey and Don Yenco. Yenco, of Canonburg, Pennsylvania, produced a Camaro conversion that could be ordered directly from Chevrolet. These featured the factory-installed iron-block L-72 engine, and are referred to as COPOs—for Central Order Production Office.

But, topping all of these limited-edition Camaros was the Baldwin Motion Phase III, featured on the following pages.

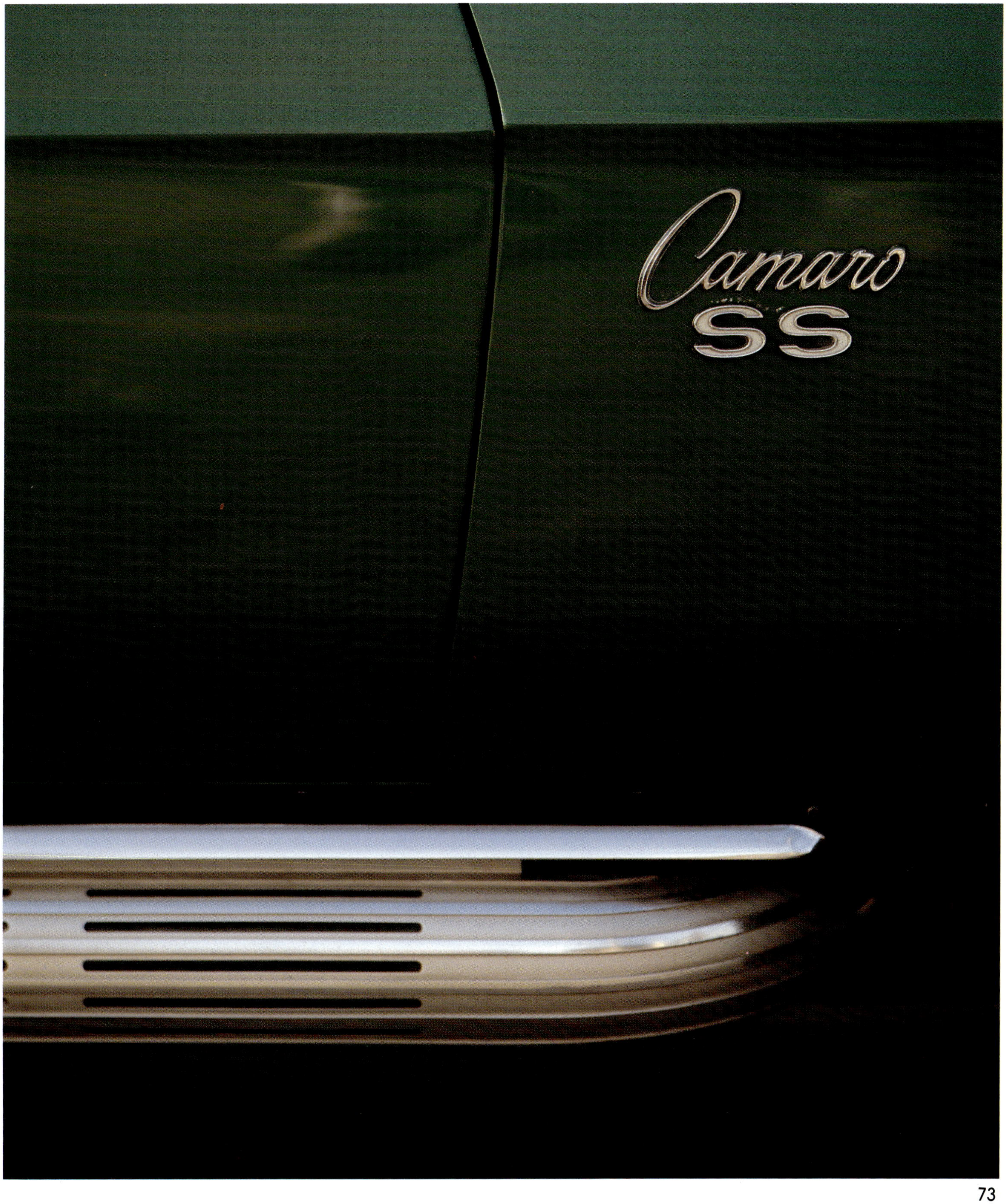
Camaro
SS

*T*he Baldwin Motion Camaro was not exactly a factory stock machine, although, on the other hand, it was certainly not a one-off custom. It could in fact be ordered through a Chevrolet dealer, and thus occupies a legitimate place in muscle car annals. The name, Baldwin, comes from the Chevrolet dealer in Baldwin, New York, from which it could be ordered. The Motion portion stems from Motion Performance, a firm headed by drag racer Joel Rosen, whose business was located just down the street from the dealership. After an order had been taken by Baldwin, a brand new Camaro would be entrusted to the able hands of Rosen, who would place an L-72 engine—dyno-tuned to produce in excess of 500 horses—in the engine bay. The suspension would also be beefed up, receiving special traction bars, calibrated shocks, spacers and stabilizer bars. The finished package could transport its driver down the quarter-mile stretch in less than 11 seconds. And the 0-60 mph time was somewhere in the mid-fours.

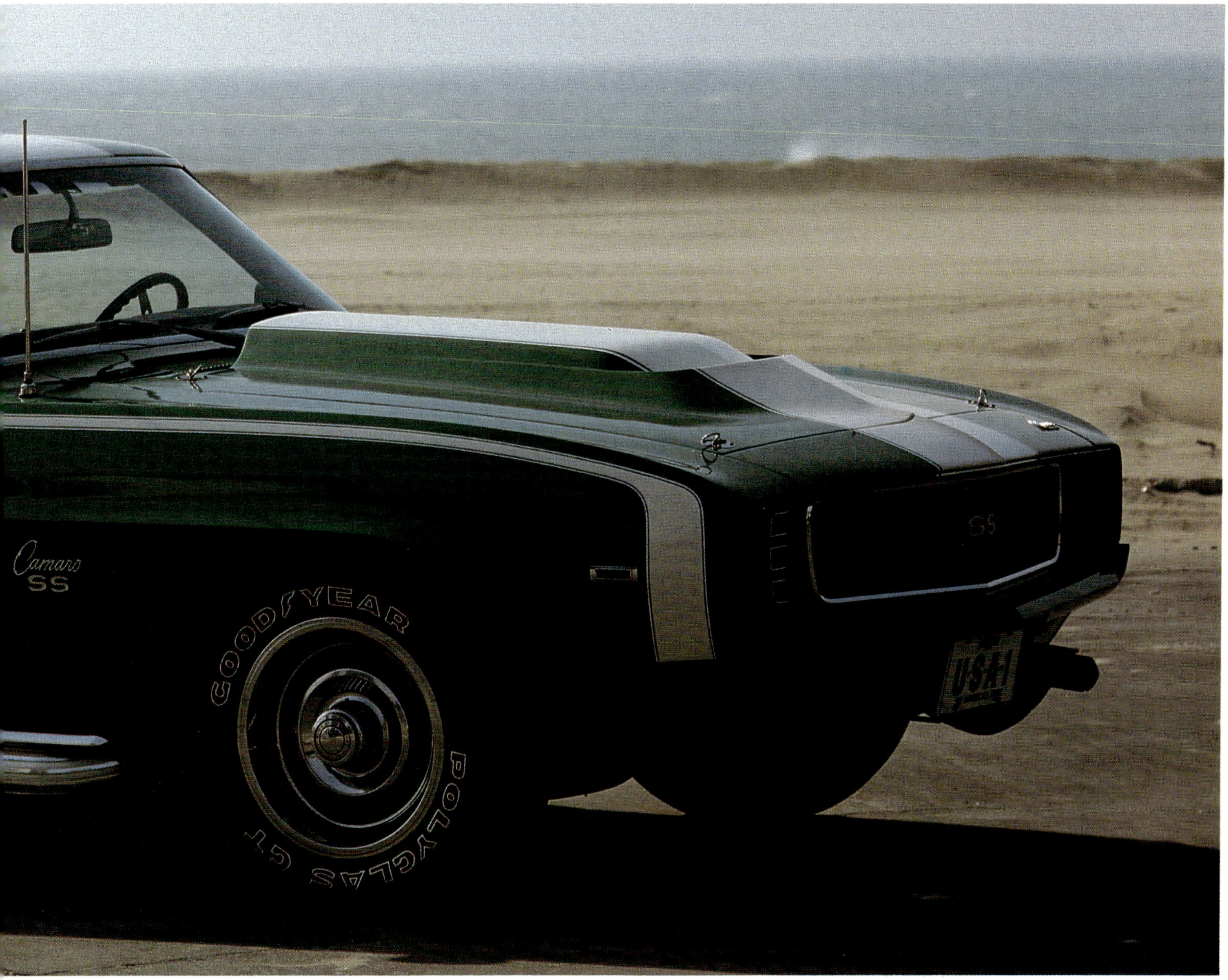
Camaro
SS
GOODYEAR
POLYGLAS GT
SS
USA-1

Here is yet another view of the Baldwin Motion, splendid in its Rally Green livery. The featured car has a unique and exciting history. While most of these machines were trashed on the drag strips, this one was purchased new by the son-in-law of the governor of Chihuahua, Mexico. A few years ago, an American with a fascination for Motion machinery managed to trace the car to its original owner. Moth-balled on his farm, it was found to be in pristine condition, with less than 6,000 miles on the clock. While it was almost impossible to spend more than $5,000 for a new Camaro, even one optioned to the maximum, this particular Baldwin Motion set the original buyer back almost twice that amount, or $8,520, a figure verified by the dealership invoice.

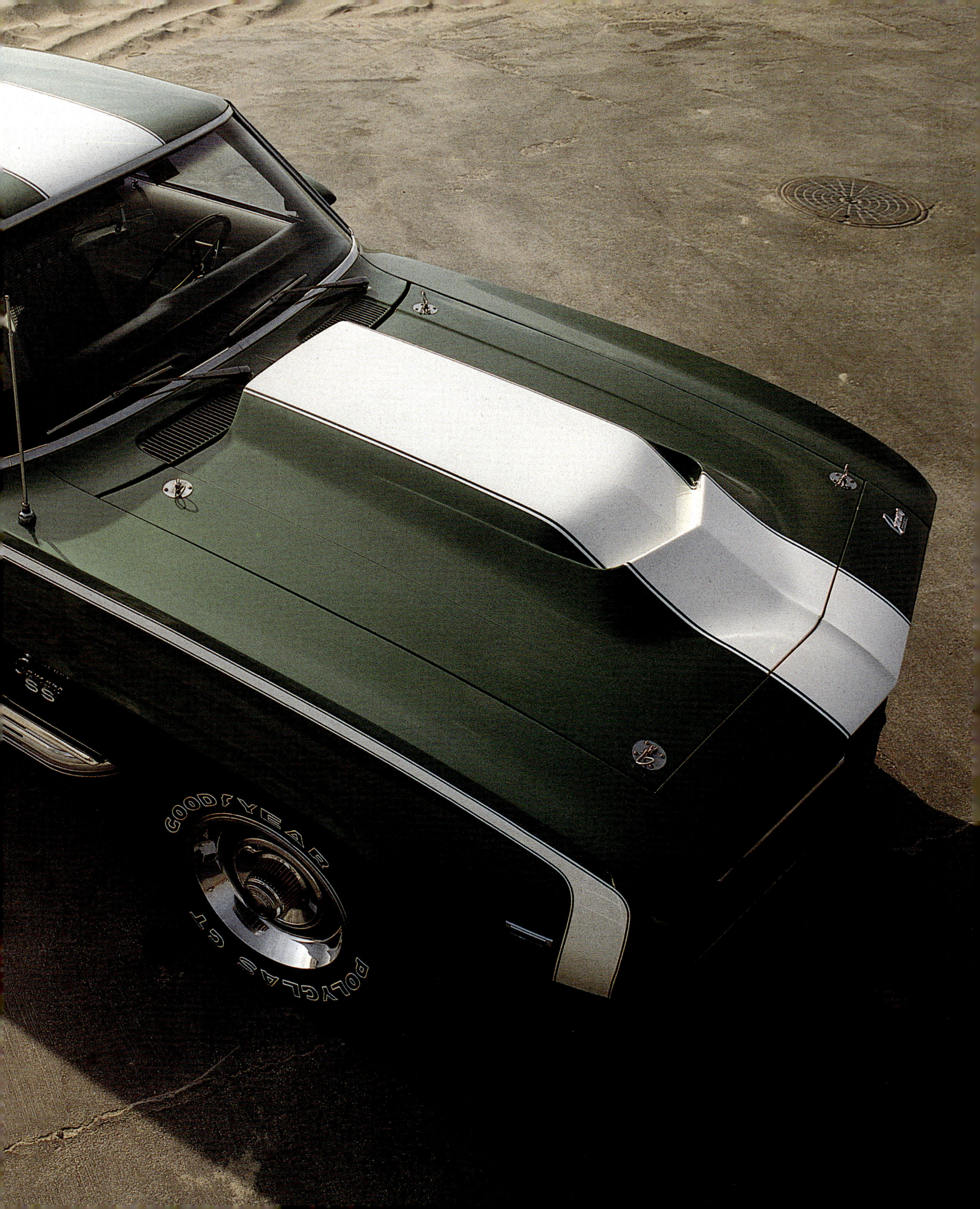
GOODYEAR
POLYGLAS GT

The rear spoiler, featured in the photograph above, came from Oldsmobile and is thought to be unique to this particular example of the Baldwin Motion Camaro. To the right, an overhead view of the heart of the matter, the L-72 engine—easy to photograph thanks to the removable fiberglass hood. When in position, the hood is secured by four racing-type lock pins. The first owner had replaced the original hoses with ones of the braided-steel type. The present owner has returned the engine compartment to stock configuration, except for the carburetor, which is a triple-barrel Holley Daytona, and the air cleaner, which is by Mr. Gasket—both items originally specified and installed by Joel Rosen and his Motion Performance. Among a host of other items installed by Rosen was a dual trunk-mounted Holley electric fuel pump system.

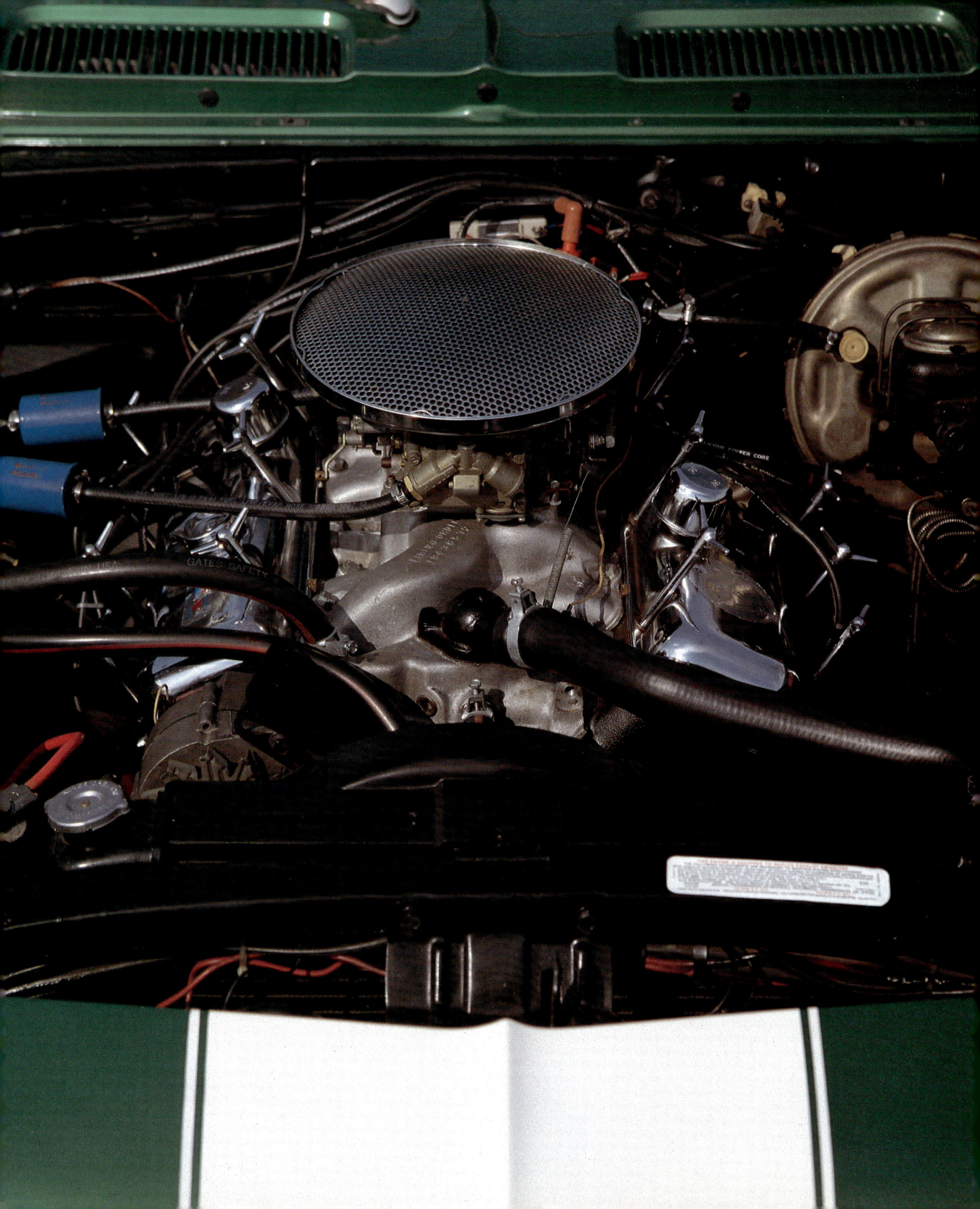
GATES SAFETY

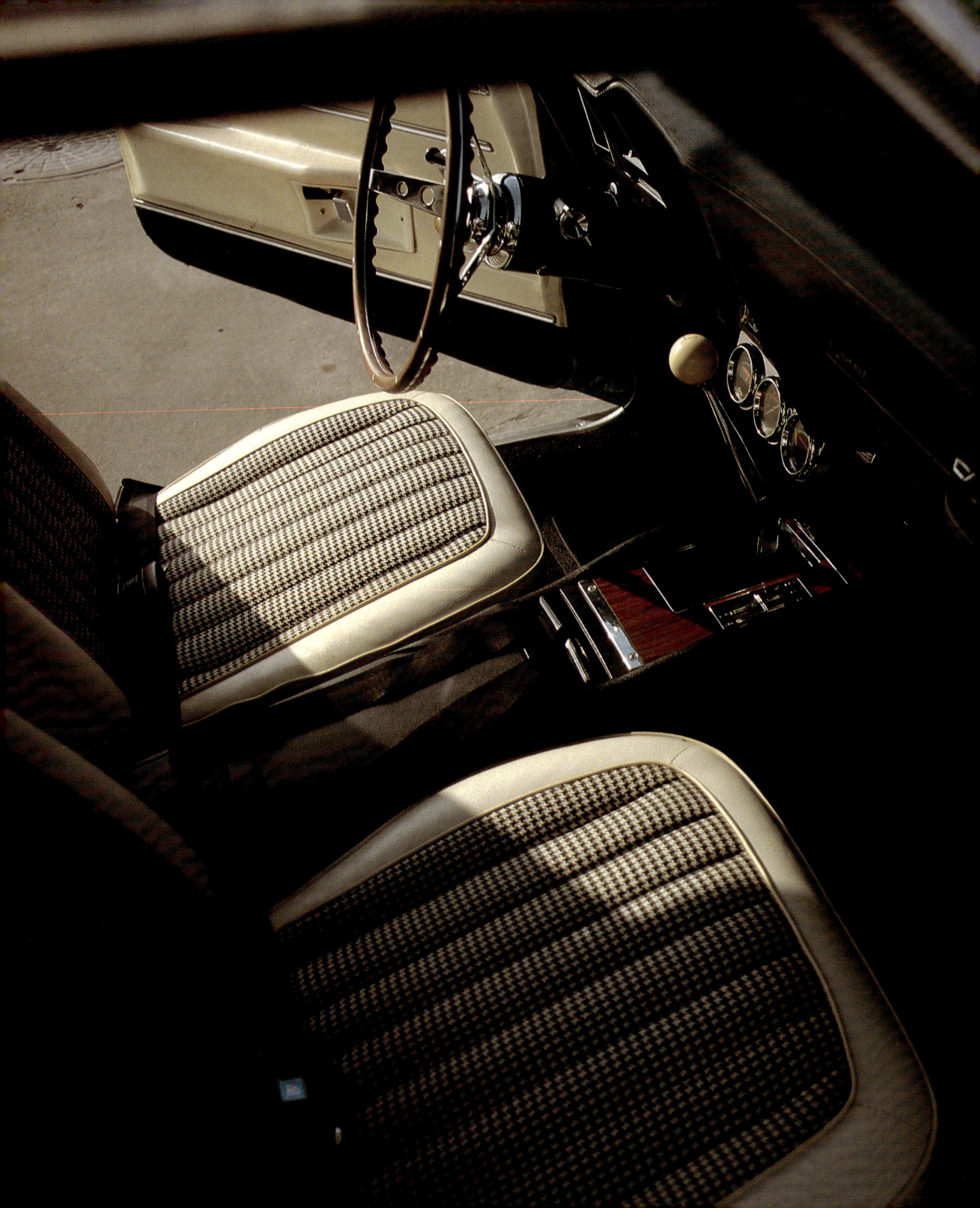

The interior of the Baldwin Motion Camaro, two decades old, still sports the original upholstery—Chevrolet's handsome optional hound's-tooth-style cloth, in "as new" condition. The wood steering wheel, mounted on a column equipped with the factory-tilt feature, was a Rosen-specified aftermarket product, as was the triple set of Sun gauges fitted under the dash, facilitating accurate monitoring of amp, oil pressure and water temperature. The Hurst shifter, with its massive knob, connected to a four-speed manual transmission. Rosen's Phase III package included the fitting of Chevrolet's 4.56:1 rear. Power was transmitted to the road via aftermarket Anson sprint wheels, wrapped in Goodyear Indy tires. The dealer invoice listed a tachometer, an item Rosen would normally have placed on the hood, but the entry had been crossed out, and the car, curiously, to this day still lacks this vital instrument—an indication that the machine might never have been raced. But that must surely be the only performance-related item this awesome machine is missing.

1970 Ford Mustang Boss 429

Mightiest of the muscle Mustangs

Mustang mating—not without a shoehorn.

Ford's 1964 introduction of the Mustang, an event that took place in midyear rather than during the customary fall season, became one of the most successful new-model launches in automotive history. Demand was so great that production, originally set to be handled by the Dearborn facility alone, had to be expanded to California and New Jersey plants.

At the end of 1964, a total of 122,000 Mustangs had been built. By the anniversary of the introduction, May 17, that number had swelled to 418,000. The year as a whole saw the completion of 559,000 units. The peak came in 1966, with a total of 608,000. Production for the entire decade of the Mustang, ending in 1973, reached three million.

As with John DeLorean and his creation of Pontiac's GTO, the executive responsible for the Mustang—Lee Iacocca—was hailed as a genius and rose rapidly to the top of the executive hierarchy. Furthermore, proving how small the inner circle of Detroit chiefs was, Semon E. "Bunkie" Knudsen, once DeLorean's boss, later moved to Ford, where he influenced the destiny of the Mustang during the autumn of its life. One of his creations was the Boss 429—mightiest of the muscle Mustangs.

The sporty character of the Mustang was at the heart of the concept from the beginning, but it became increasingly emphasized as the muscle car craze progressed. While there was always a six-cylinder choice at the base of the performance ladder, only a minority opted for this alternative.

The gap between performance extremes actually widened. In 1964, the 170 ci six produced 101 hp, and the top-of-the-line 289 ci V-8 Challenger put out 271 hp. In 1970, the 200 ci Maverick six produced 120 hp, while the 429 ci Boss was listed at 375 hp—although the actual figure was much higher.

At the end of the Mustang era, the 250 ci six produced an anemic 88 hp, and the 351 ci Cleveland generated only 154 hp. But this was all symptomatic of the sickness that spread like a plague throughout muscle machinery in the early seventies. However, in 1970—in the form of the fabulous Boss 429—performance was still in the driver's seat.

The Boss 429 came into existence solely to improve Ford's racing program. The Hemi-powered Plymouths were wreaking havoc on the NASCAR circuit, and, instead of trying to beat the opposition, Ford decided to join it by producing its own Hemi—the 429. In order to meet the homologation demands, 500 units had to be built, so Knudsen ordered the huge motor shoehorned into the small Mustang.

The 429 powerplant was so massive that a special assembly line had to be organized to execute mandated changes to the suspension, which among other measures included moving the upper and lower A-arms outward.

With a price tag of $4,798, a hefty sum in those days, the Boss 429 was still a bargain—especially when one adds two decades of steady increases in both historic and monetary appreciation. Just 858 cars were built in 1969. For 1970, the year of the example on the following pages, the figure was 498—making this a rare beast indeed.

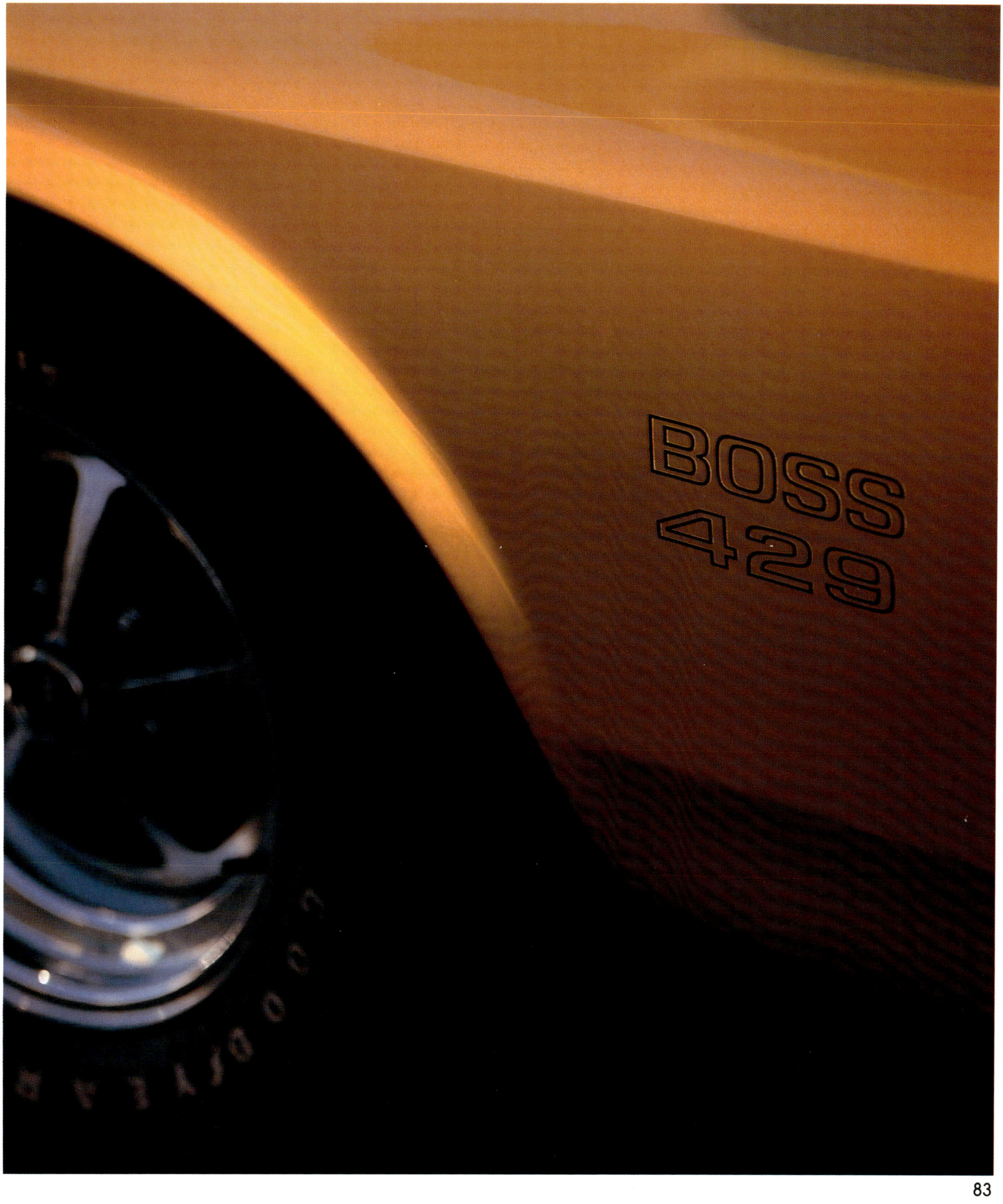
BOSS
429

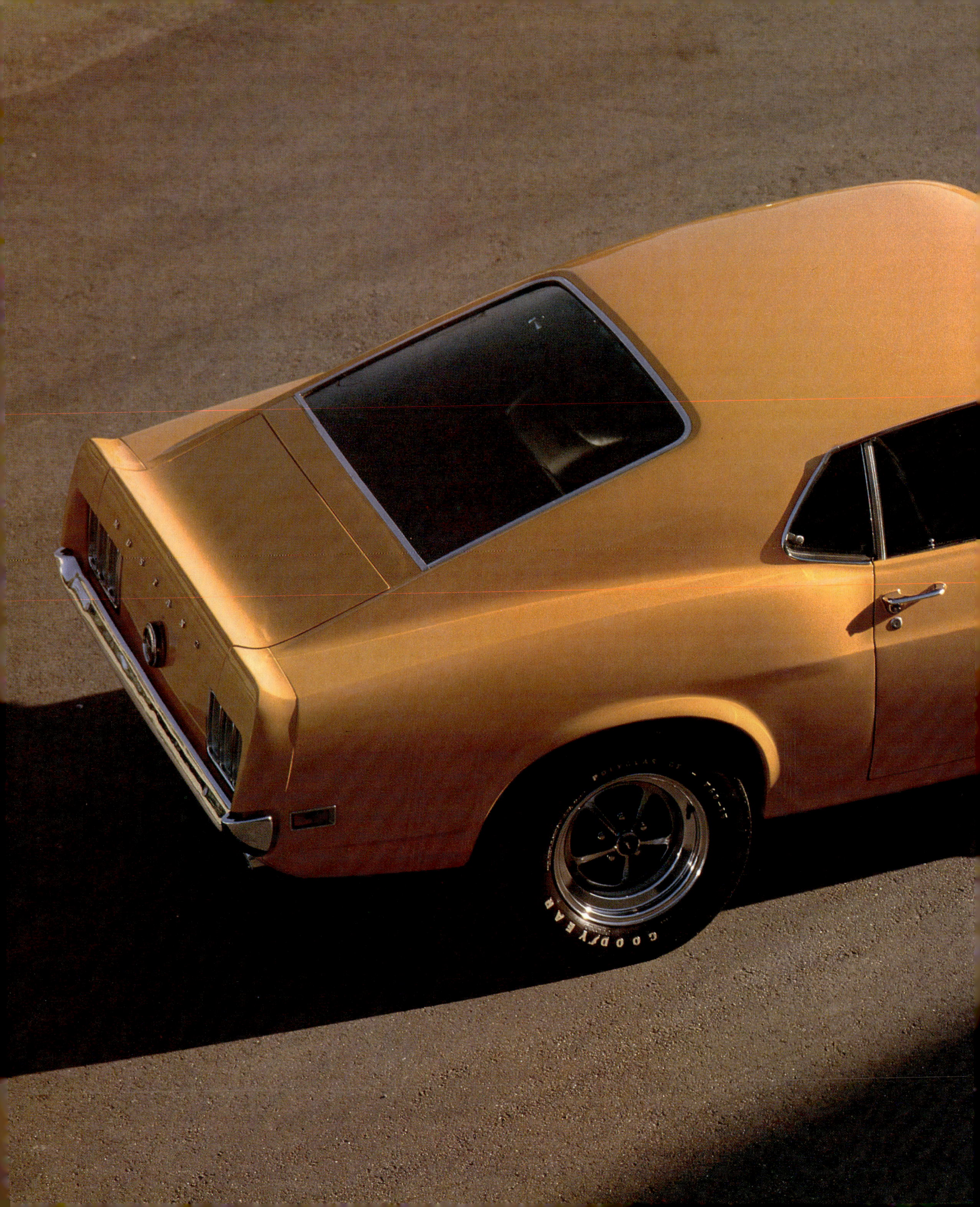

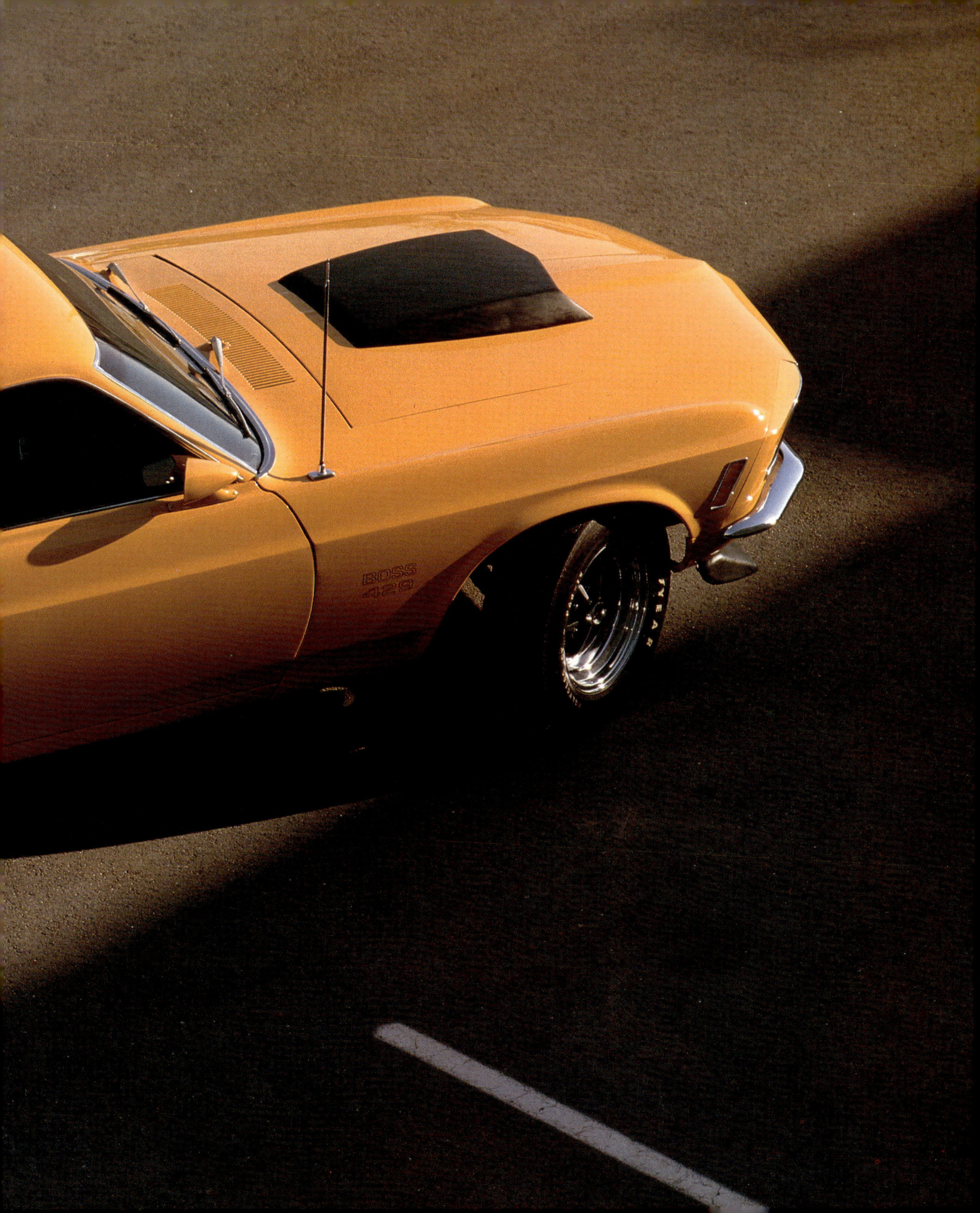
BOSS
429

The Boss was not bellicose. Only a simple decal hinted of the latent power hiding beneath the Grabber Orange surface, as shown on the opening pages of this chapter. The Boss utilized the Sportroof version of the Mustang—a fastback design that had received a number of styling revisions for 1969. The bird's-eye views on the previous page and the following page illustrate efforts undertaken to modernize a style that had grown weary. The roofline appeared more sweeping than ever, and the in-motion look was further accentuated by the crease running from the front, skirting the flared wheelwell and shooting toward the back of the body. The side panels were otherwise clean and simple, and the entire car was nearly void of chrome decorations. Seen here, the black scoop is the only object to have been singled out for accentuation.

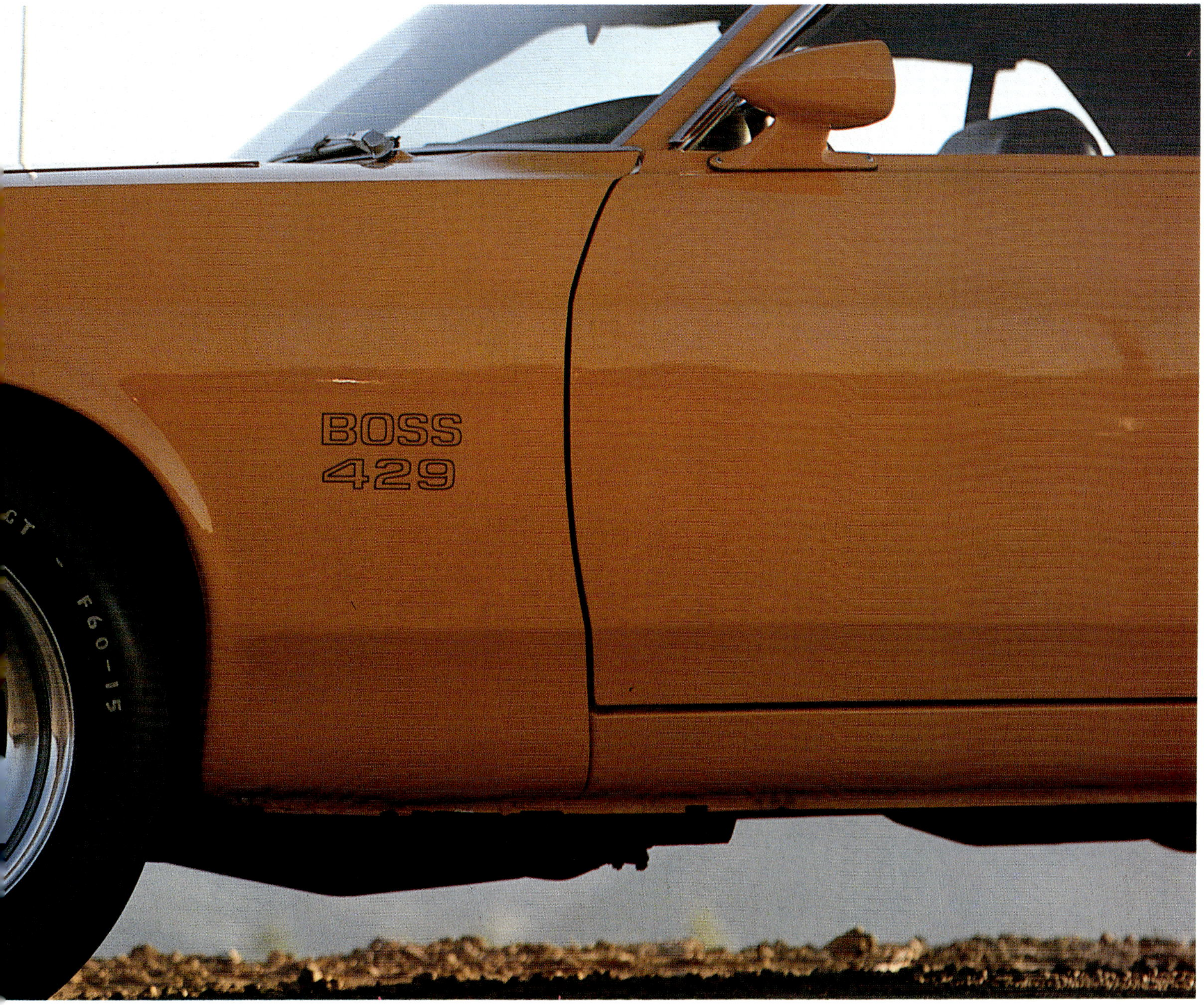
BOSS
429
F60-15

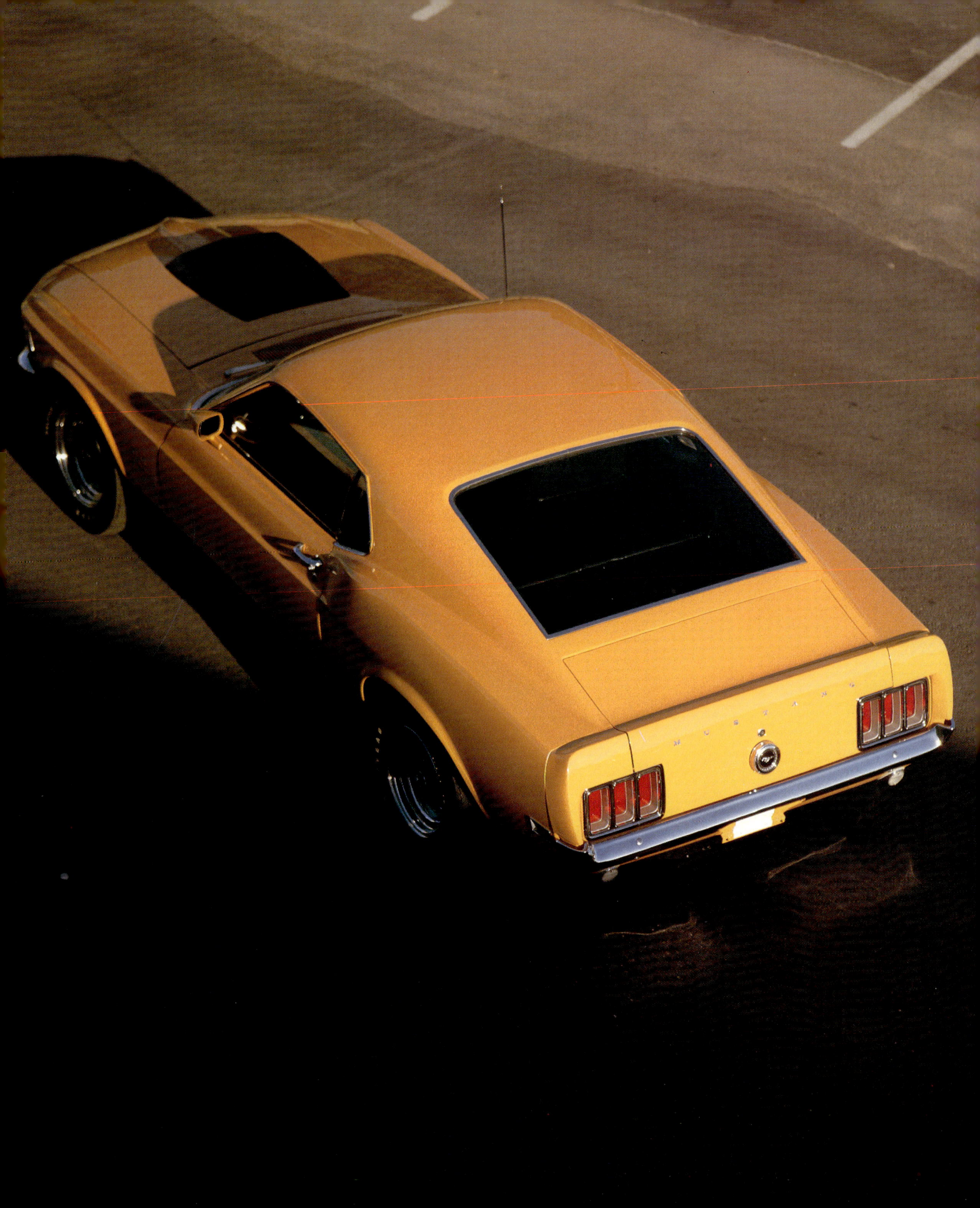

Pictured above, an under-hood view of the 429 Boss. Below the air cleaner hid a four-barrel Holley. And below this wide-mouthed contraption rested a special aluminum intake manifold, flanked by the cylinder heads with their Hemi-configured combustion chambers, also of aluminum. The stated—but underrated—output of 375 hp was reached at 5200 rpm. Coupled to the potent package was a close-ratio four-speed manual transmission, terminating in a standard 3.91:1 Traction-Lok differential. Power was transmitted to the pavement via seven-inch Magnum 500 chrome wheels, as seen on the previous page. This photograph also allows a look at the front spoiler, a crucially important aerodynamic aid that prevented lift at high speeds. Zero to 60 mph took less than 7.1 seconds. The quarter-mile was covered in 14.09 seconds.

1970 Dodge Challenger R/T 426 Hemi

Late-comer captures the laurels

The R/T was the hottest Challenger around.

The Challenger was Dodge's much-delayed, but definitive entry in the pony car race. By 1970 the field had become fiercely crowded; featured in addition to Ford's original trendsetter—the aging Mustang—were Mercury's Cougar, Chevrolet's Camaro, Pontiac's Firebird and Plymouth's Barracuda. American Motors' AMX, although a two-seater, was also a contender.

When the Mustang arrived in 1964, Plymouth had already unveiled its first-generation Barracuda. From the timing—the new Plymouth was introduced on April 1, seventeen days ahead of the Mustang—it was evident that the marketing people at Plymouth had been thinking along the same lines as the folks at Ford. The result was far from definitive, however; the Barracuda lacked the degree of sportiness found in the Mustang.

With the Challenger, all that changed. The new styling was fully in tune with the pony car concept. It appeared that Dodge's entry had benefited from the delay—the Challenger was a beautifully balanced design, with a short rear deck and a long hood. The lines were rounded and the upturned sweep given to the lower portions of the front and rear created a feeling of flight.

The Challenger was available in two basic configurations: the standard and the R/T. Each was broken down into three body styles—hardtop, convertible and SE hardtop—the latter sporting a vinyl roof with a small window in the sail panel.

Power also came in a variety of combinations. The bottom choice was a 225 ci six, producing 145 hp. Next came a 318 ci V-8, generating 230 hp. A 340 ci V-8 was another option. Fitted with four-barrel carburetion, this engine had an output of 275 hp. A 383 ci unit, breathing through a twin-barrel carburetor, produced 290 hp. Equipped with a four-barrel carburetor, output increased to 330 hp.

Standard power in the R/T version came from the 383 ci unit, rated at 335 hp. Optional power was derived from a 440 ci, rated at 375 hp. The 440 unit was also available equipped with three twin-barrel carburetors—the famous Six Pack—with an output of 390 hp.

But the real screamer was the 426 Hemi. Gulping air through twin four-barrel carburetors, this super-potent machine produced 425 hp at 5600 rpm. The price tag for such shattering performance was a mere $779 on top of the R/T's base sticker of $3,266.

Total production of the 1970 Challenger was 83,032 units, counting all variations on the theme. Most common was the basic hardtop, which sold to the tune of 53,337 units. The SE attracted 6,584 buyers.

The hardtop R/T added up to a total of 14,899 units. The R/T SE was the option of only 3,979. And again, the convertible was opted for by just 1,070 wind-in-the-hair die-hards, making it the most unique of the three Challenger body styles.

Challenger

R/T

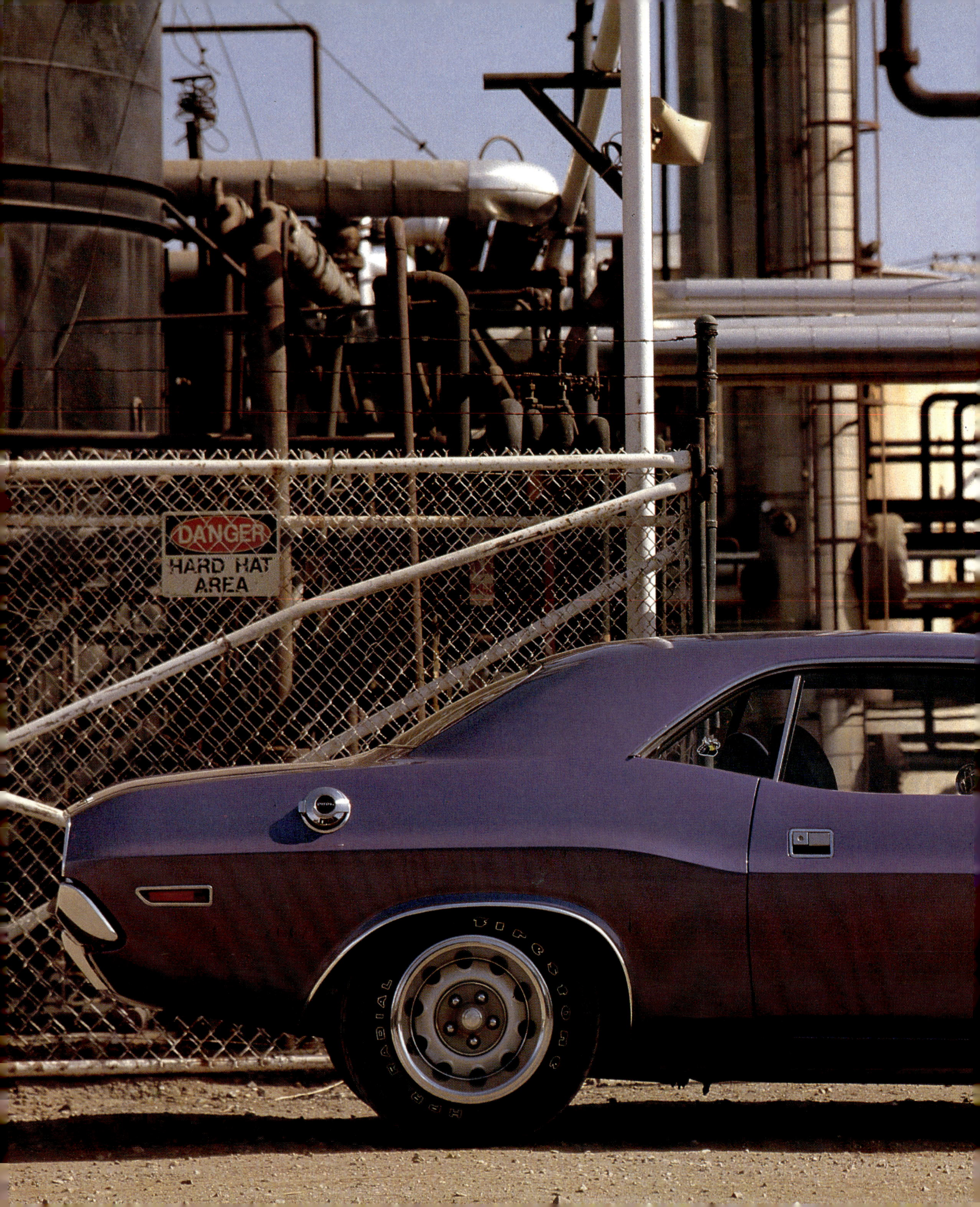
DANGER
HARD HAT
AREA

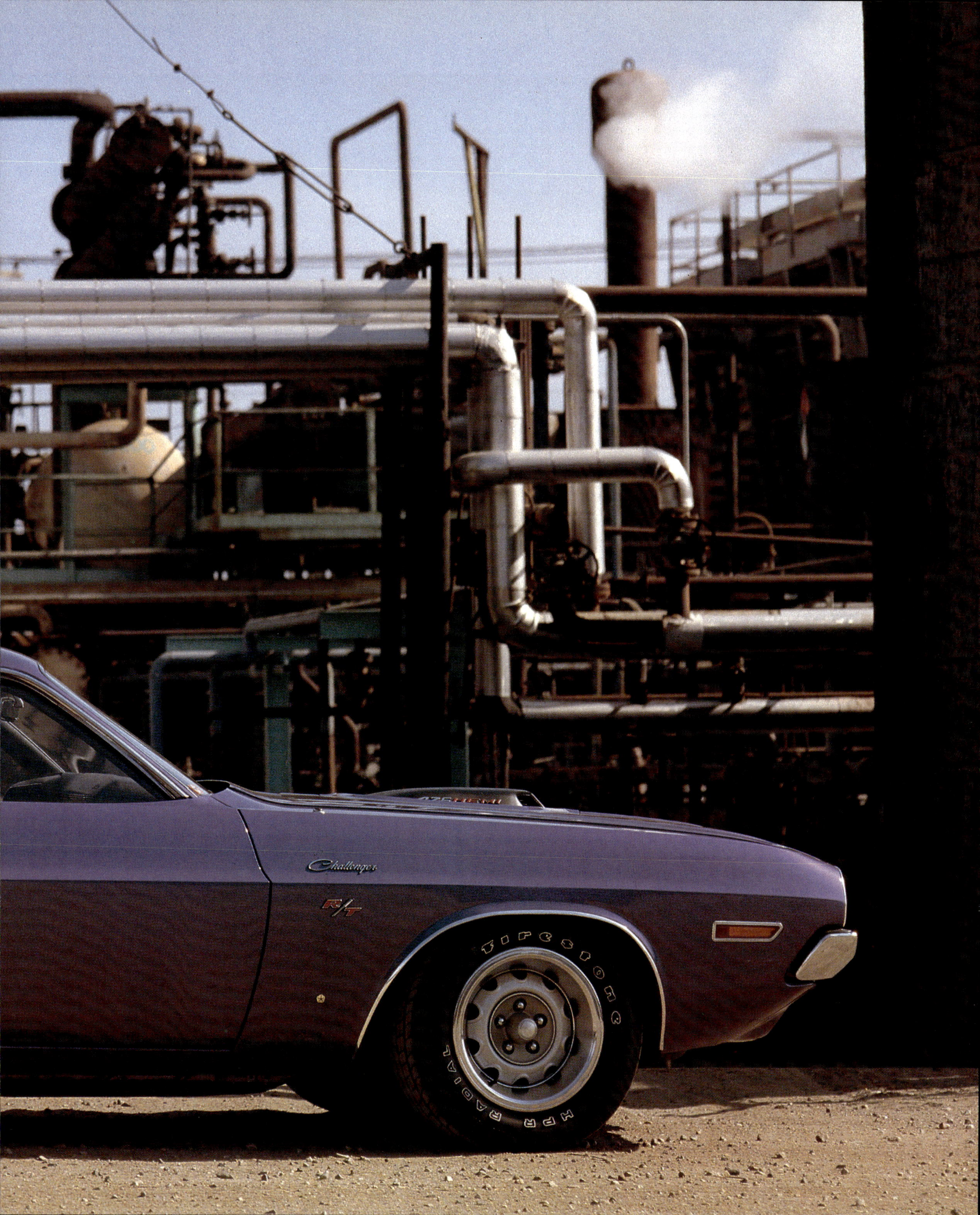
Challenger
R/T
Firestone
HPR RADIAL

In profile, as pictured on the previous page, the appealing visual balance of the Challenger can be fully appreciated. Appearing longer and lower than its competitors in the pony car field, Dodge's entry was quite a feather in the stylist's hat. The side panels were clean and simple. A single crease repeated the basic outline of the car, with its raised rear quarters. The low-cut and nicely curved wheelwells were in an eyebrow-like shape accentuated by a thin chrome lip mounted on the edge of a subtle flair. The decorative Rallye wheels were optional on the base model, but were included in the R/T package. The rear of the Challenger, in the photograph above, repeated the shape of the front, with a recessed, full-width taillight assembly. A straight-on view of the Challenger, on the following page, made for a most aggressive image—the potent machine appeared to hug the ground in jealous fervor. The wide tires added further emphasis to this sure-footed stance.

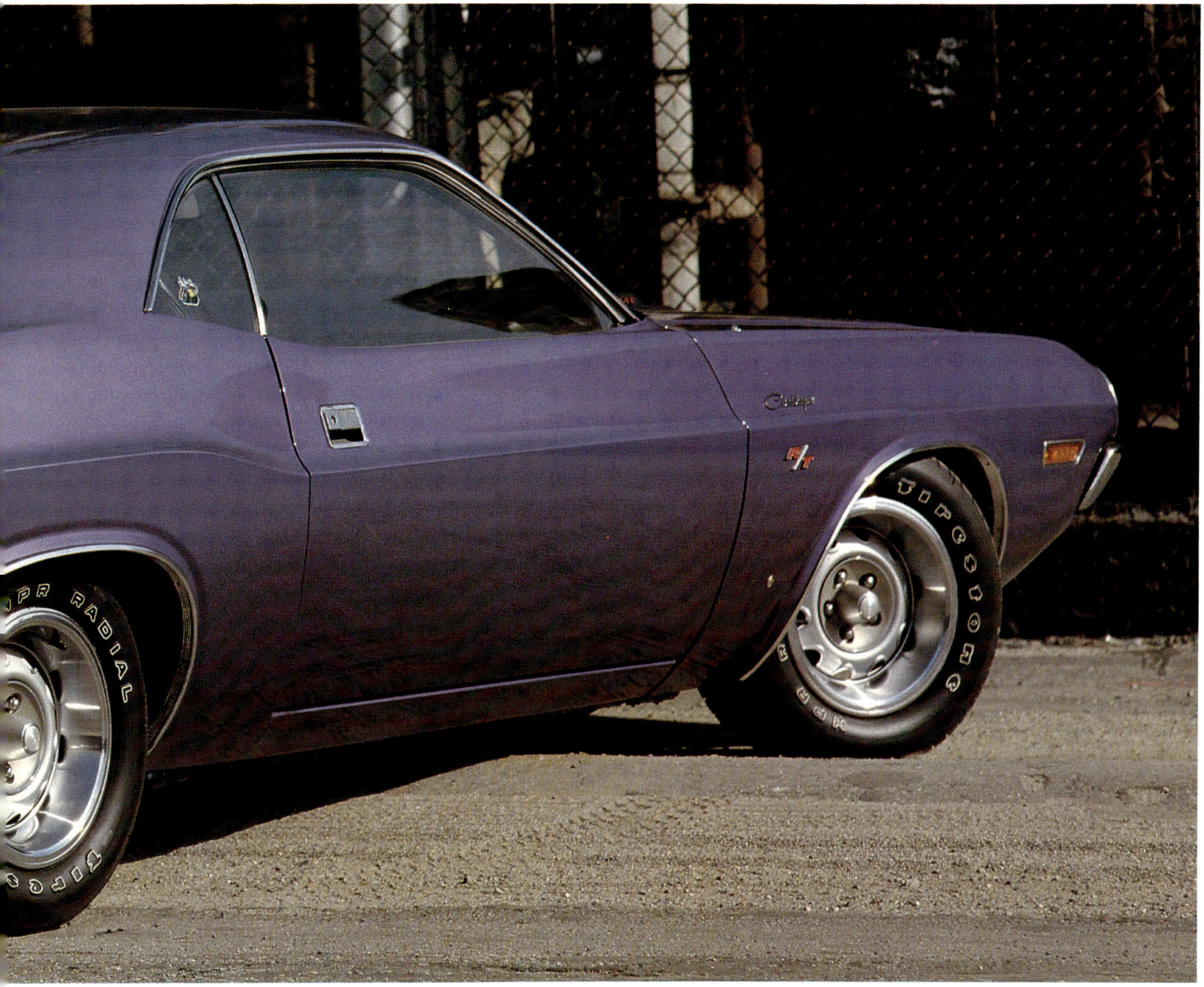
HPR RADIAL

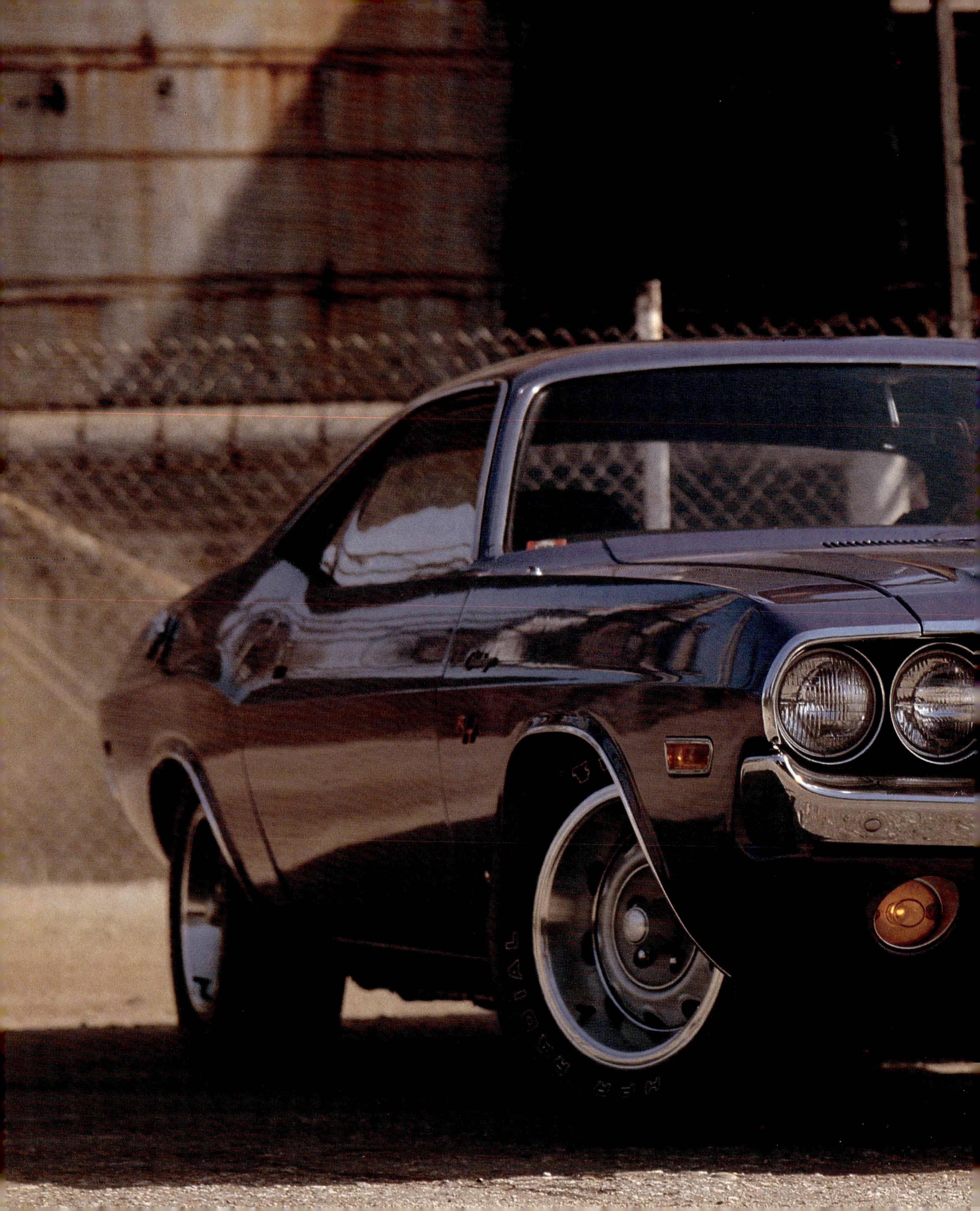

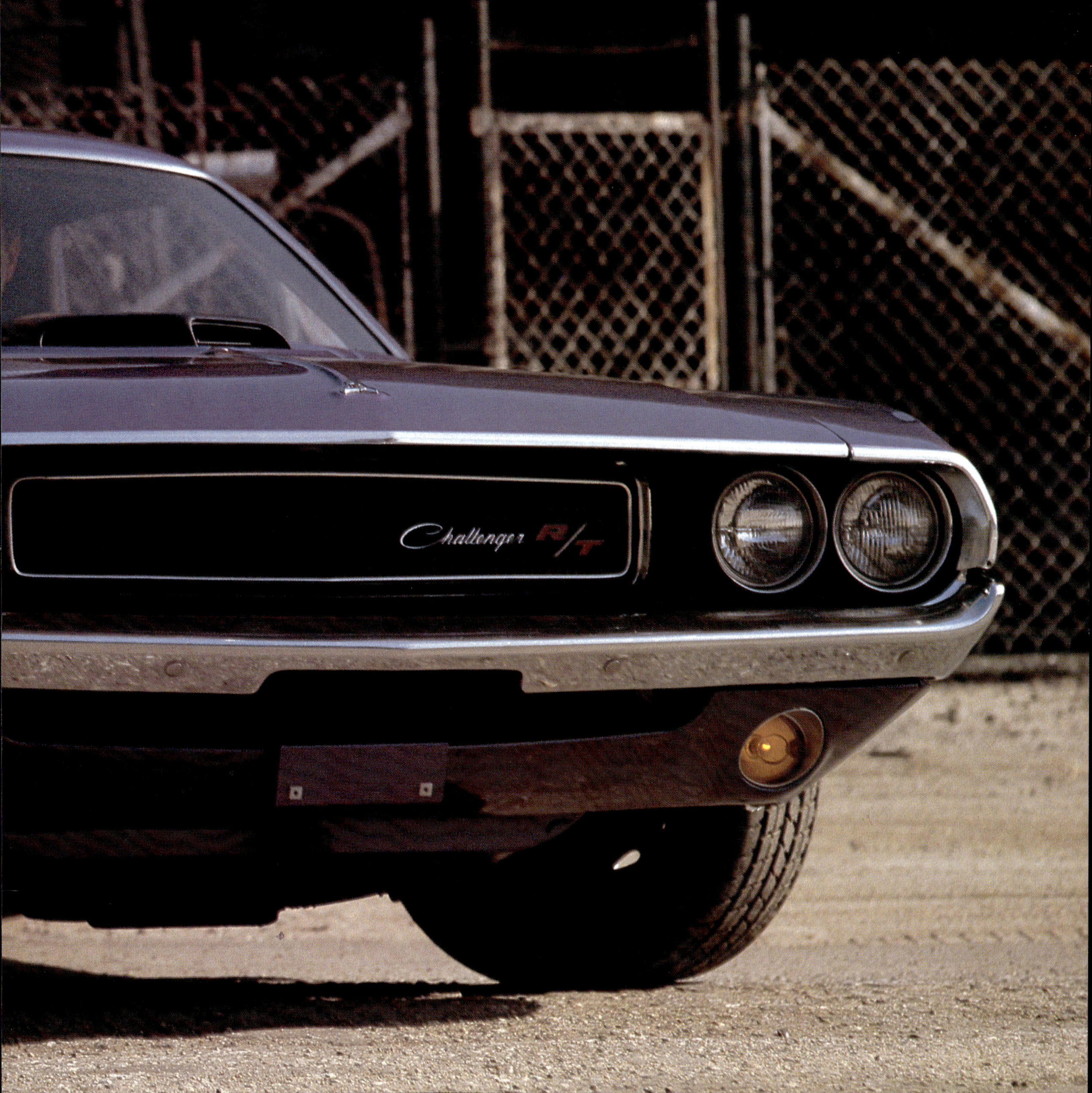
Challenger R/T

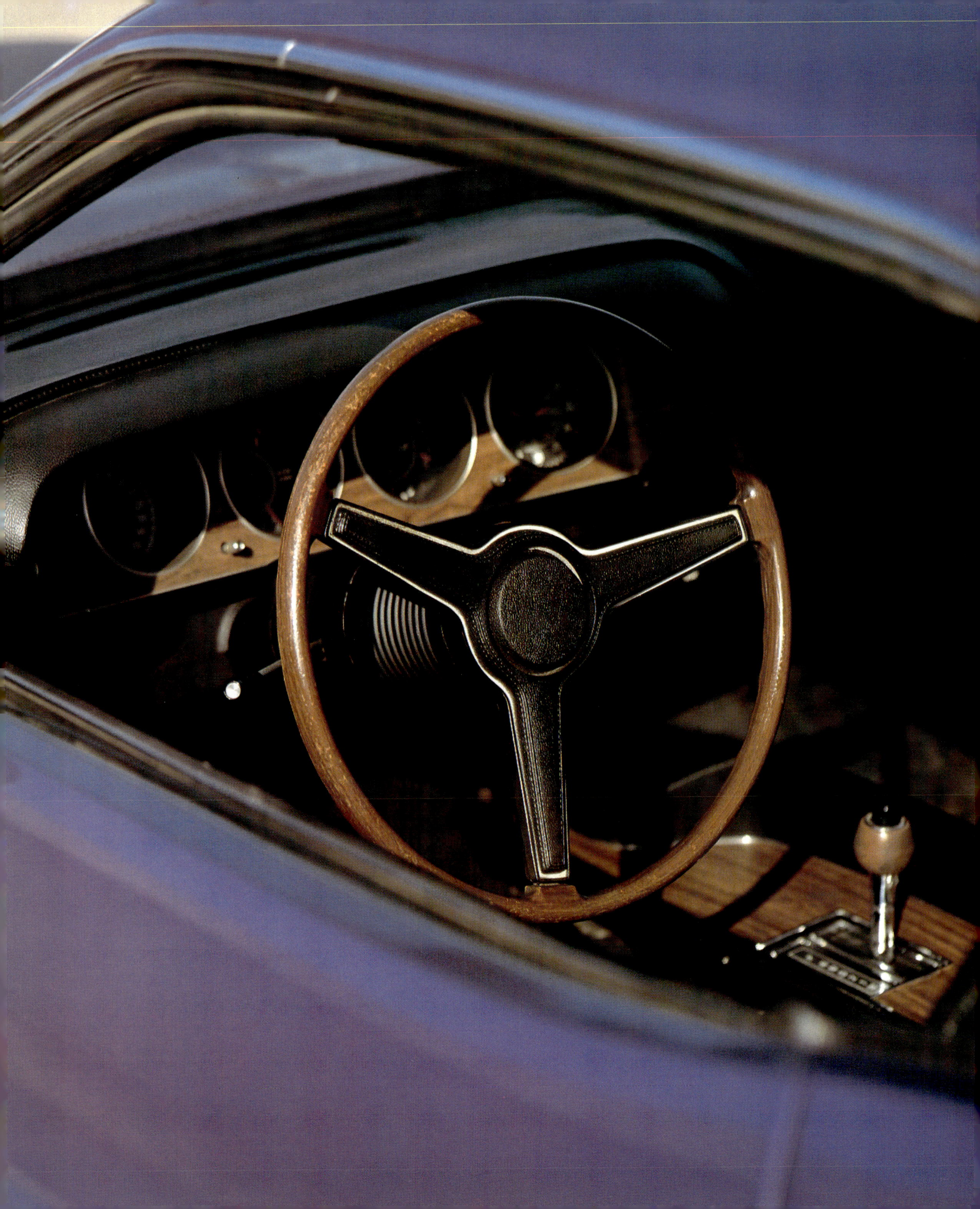

In their efforts to give the Challenger an image worthy of all that power under the hood, Dodge stylists let their imagination run free, although not to the point of the absurd. Pictured to the left, the shape of the steering wheel spokes is delicately accentuated by a fine white edge. Pictured above, a feature that was certain to catch the attention of the performance set—the Shaker hood scoop option. This unit, protruding through an opening in the hood, was actually an extension of the air cleaner, and mounted directly on top of the carburetors. The scoop, as executed, may not have had a practical purpose, but the sight of that engine extension—shivering from brutish emotion—certainly provided an intriguing viewing interlude every time the driver was caught at a traffic light. The Challenger, equipped with the Hemi, covered the 0-60 mph distance in 5.8 seconds, and the quarter-mile in 14.1 seconds.

1970 Plymouth Road Runner Superbird

Winged monster of NASCAR eminence

Ready to fly—freshly hatched Superbirds.

In 1970, readers of *Hot Rod* magazine's February issue were intrigued by a daring double-page ad, featuring a photograph of a winged monster of a car. The setting was decidedly "down home"—outlaw country even—with a collection of rugged individuals gathered around the machine. The headline, announcing "a new kind of Runner," explained in a not-so-subtle way what Lightning Billy was actually up to—in the background, the viewer could see the outline of a contraption looking suspiciously like a whiskey still.

There was no doubt as to the target of the ad—the South, where NASCAR racing was very popular. Plymouth had been the undisputed winner in 1967, scoring firsts in thirty-one out of forty-nine races. And if NASCAR was dominated by Plymouth, Richard Petty, who had amassed both wins and wealth, was its king.

The effect on sales was no secret. Why else would the manufacturers bother? Those who were in a position to study sales reports in regions most affected by this kind of racing could testify that on a Monday morning after a big Sunday win, the winning models moved at a decidedly quicker pace in the showroom.

Later, when Plymouth took a breather from racing, Petty went to Ford. Then, for the 1970 season, Plymouth, which by that time had decided to join the fray again, wanted to lure its number-one chauffeur back to the fold. But he needed some assurances. The Superbird was the answer.

This brute was based on the 1969 Dodge Charger 500, and the Charger Daytona; the latter broke 200 mph at Dodge's test track. To meet homologation rules, Dodge had been required to build a minimum of 500 units of both the Charger 500 and the Daytona.

The Daytona was based on aerodynamic experiments performed on the original 1966 Charger and was initially tested at Goodyear's circular San Angelo track in Texas. Come race day, the Charger turned out to be impossible to control on the sharper turns of the Daytona oval. Subsequent wind tunnel testing at Wichita State University indicated that rear-end lift was indeed a problem.

In 1968 arrived the major restyling of the Dodge and Plymouth B-bodies.

By the time the Superbird was ready to be put into production, the rules committee had changed the game again—now they called for the manufacturer to build one for every other dealer. Thus, the Superbird was duplicated 1,920 times. Many collectors realized the significance of the occasion, and bought an example to put away for posterity.

The particular copy featured on these pages is such a machine. With the dealer sticker still on the window—showing a bottom line of $4,884—and with just 429 miles on the clock, this Superbird is a true time capsule, recalling one of the greatest moments of the muscle car era.

101

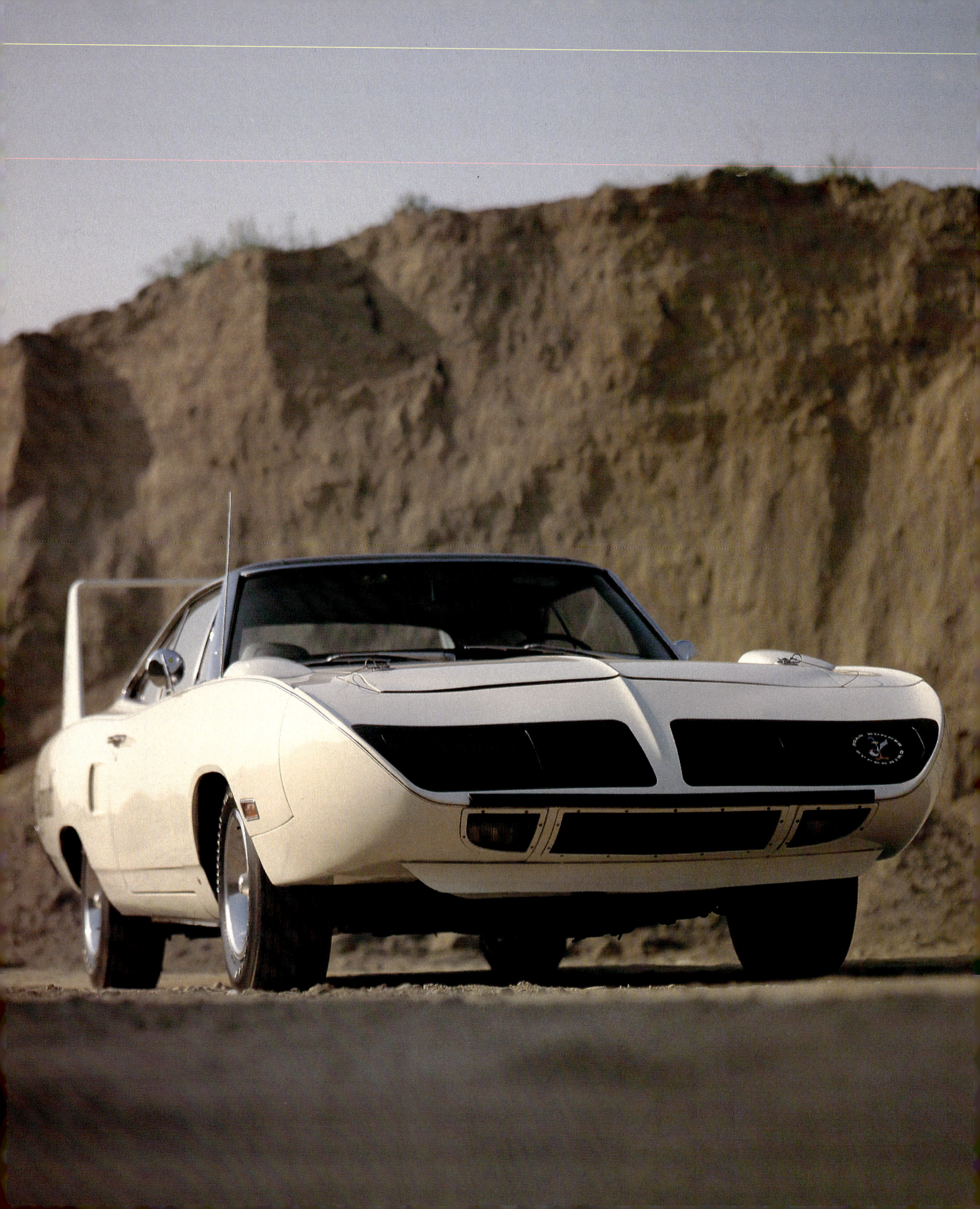

The Superbird decal, on the previous page, did not feature checkered flags or other such classic elements, but the Road Runner character was certainly perfect for the purpose. Pictured to the left, the Superbird's beak—or nose extension—added 18 inches to the overall length, which measured an impressive 218 inches. The nose also allowed room for the pop-up headlights. Cooling air was funneled through the intake under the extension. Above and on the following page, the Superbird's rear spoiler had its vertical stabilizer area increased 40 percent more than on the unit fitted to the Daytona. This helped to improve stability at high speed—for high speed was what it was all about. None of the aerodynamic aids, however, could be said to have any effect under normal driving. The spoiler might begin to work around 80 mph, but the full advantage would not be felt until around 130 mph.

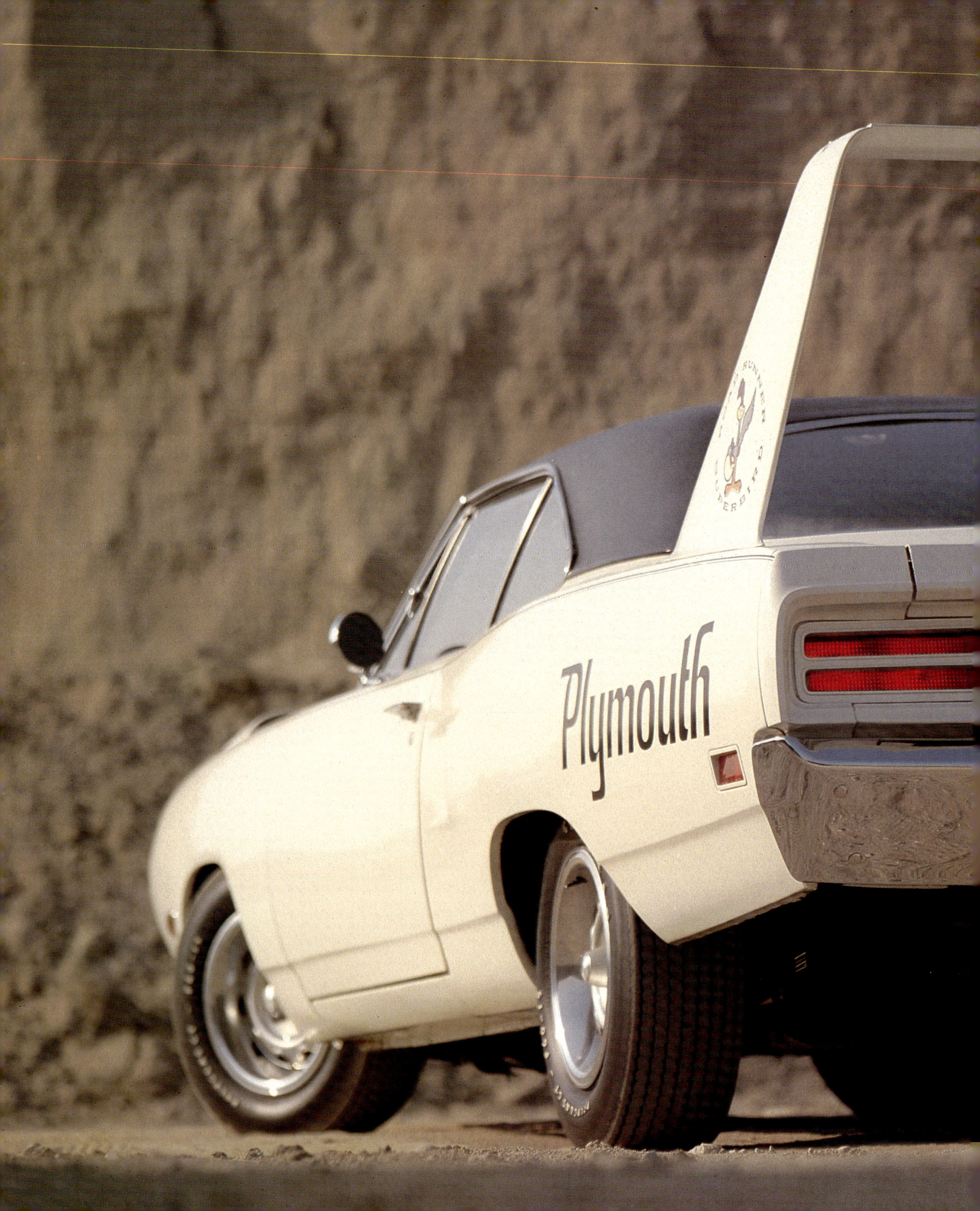
Plymouth

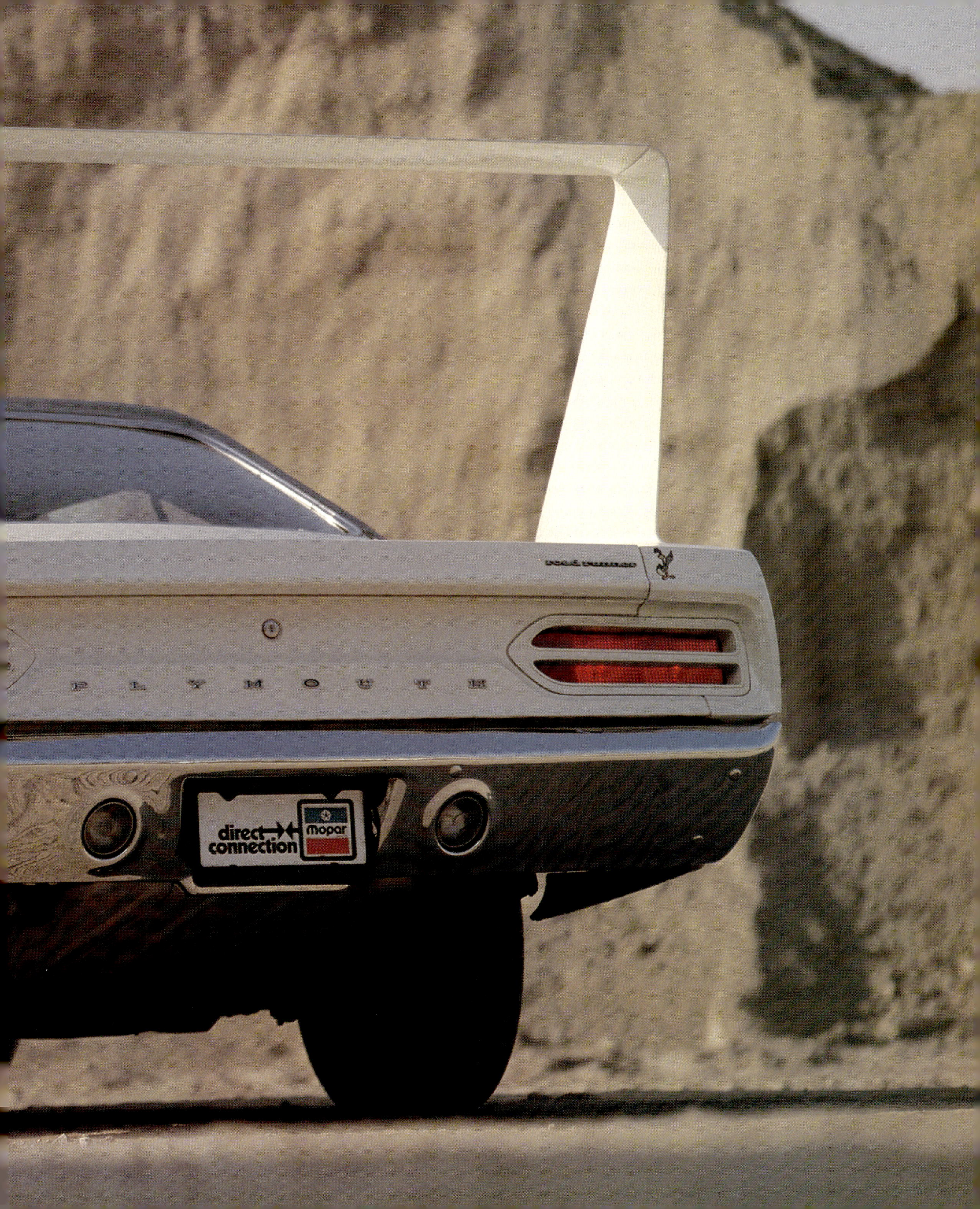

PLYMOUTH
direct connection
mopar

The interior of the street Superbird, pictured above, was every bit as comfortable as a regular road car. But the ride was pretty stiff, and every surface inconsistency could be felt. Also, because of the lack of sound deadening, the noise level was high. The tachometer was optional and missing from the particular example shown here. The TorqueFlite transmission was operated through a lever located on the console. The Superbird for the street came with three engine options. One, the 440 ci Wedge with a single four-barrel carburetor, produced 375 hp at 4600 rpm. Two, the 440 ci Wedge with the three twin-barrel Six Pack setup, seen to the right, produced 390 hp. And, three, the 426 Hemi, generating 425 hp. Even the slowest of the three was capable of covering the quarter-mile in less than 14 seconds.

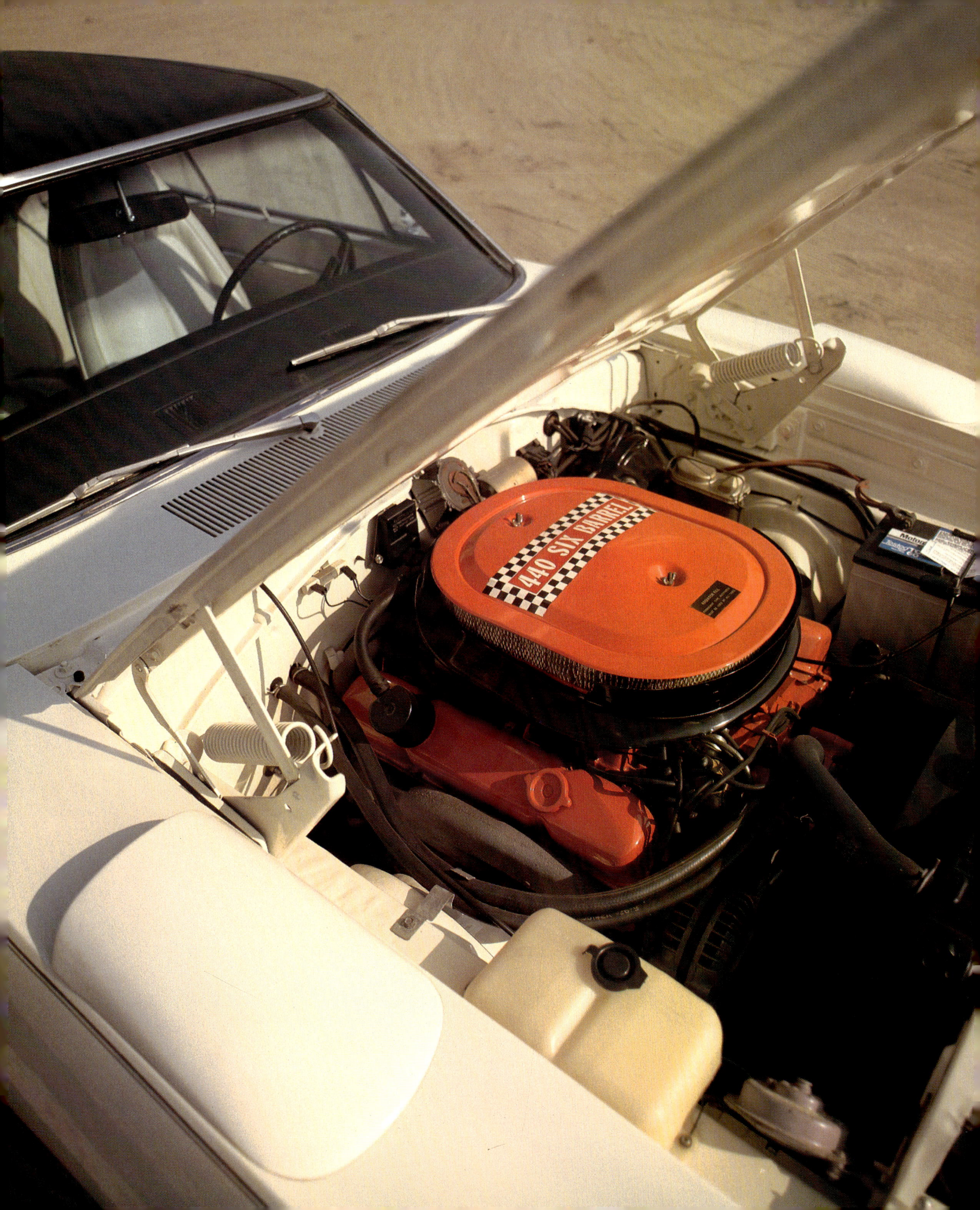
440 SIX BARREL

1970 Buick Gran Sport GSX Stage I

Packing both power and pizzazz

First year for new GS-400 style: 1968.

In the early postwar era, the Buicks, big and bulbous—and distinctive looking with their trademark toothy grilles and sporty portholes—became favorites of a car-buying public long on optimism and short on self-discipline. The touch of sportiness found in the Buicks of this period was simply a matter of styling. In the early sixties, the machines had become rather heavy, second-level luxury cars.

With the 1963 introduction of the Riviera, one of the most outstanding designs to emerge from this generation, Buick again became a style leader. The image was that of personal luxury. But as the tastes of younger buyers became more of an influence in the marketplace, sportiness became more of a concern to Buick. Enter the Gran Sport.

The Gran Sport lettering first appeared on the 1965 Riviera. Powered by a 425 ci engine developing 360 hp, the sportiness was honest and real—to the tune of 7.7 seconds 0-60 mph. The advertising executives, as usual, expressed the consequence of these figures in a more exuberant manner—the Riviera Gran Sport became "the iron fist in a velvet glove."

But the Riviera, weighing more than 4,000 pounds, was too heavy to fit the formula of a true muscle car, and so for 1966, the Gran Sport badge was extended to Buick's mid-size Skylark as well. With a weight of 3,428 pounds, a 401 ci V-8 producing 325 hp, simulated scoops, painted stripes and blacked-out grille, this machine possessed real muscle as well as styling to match.

Buick's general manager described the Gran Sport as "a completely engineered performance car," while the promoters called it "a howitzer with windshield wipers." The 0-60 mph time was improved slightly over the Riviera's, to 7.4 seconds. The quarter-mile could be covered in a respectable 14.13 seconds.

In 1967, the Skylark Gran Sport became the GS 400, so designated after its 400 ci engine. This new powerplant produced 340 hp at 5000 rpm, and was optionally coupled to Buick's three-speed variable-pitch Super-Turbine transmission. Three body styles were available: two-door hardtop—the most popular—thin-pillar coupe and convertible.

For 1968, the GS took on a new look, adopting the basic corporate body style introduced across the board that year. There was also added excitement available in the engine compartment—the dealer-installed Stage I Special Package. This included a special cam, higher compression, special pistons, stronger valve springs and changed carburetor calibration. The rating was 345 hp at 4800 rpm.

For 1969, basic styling was unchanged, although a new grille was incorporated. Then, in 1970, came the climax of the Gran Sport era—the GSX. Under the hood was the biggest engine ever, a 455 ci giant, generating 350 hp at 4600 rpm. In their Stage I and II form, these Buicks were unique—only 678 units were built—and stand out as some of the most formidable performers of the line-up in 1970, a peak year for the muscle car.

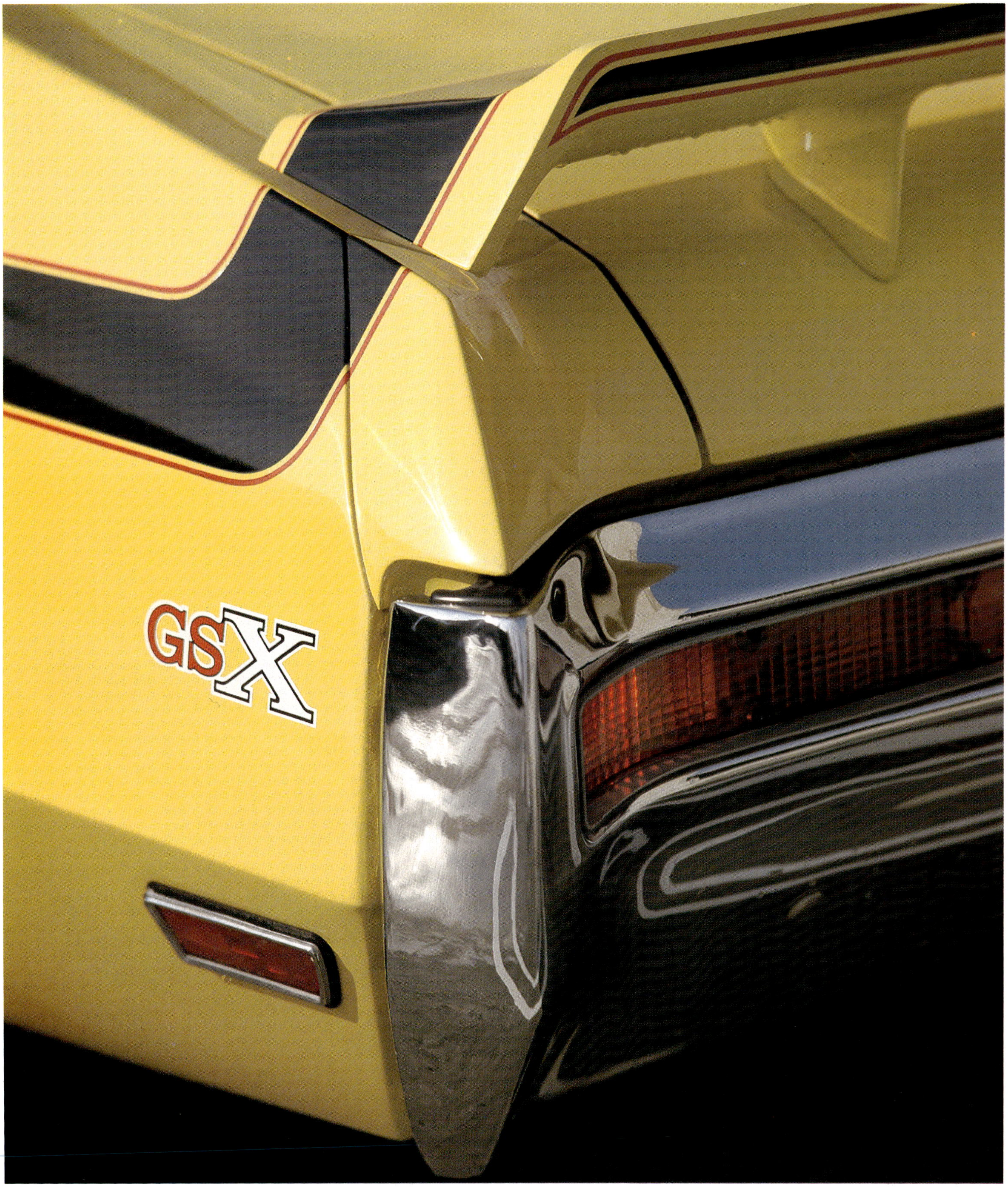
GSX

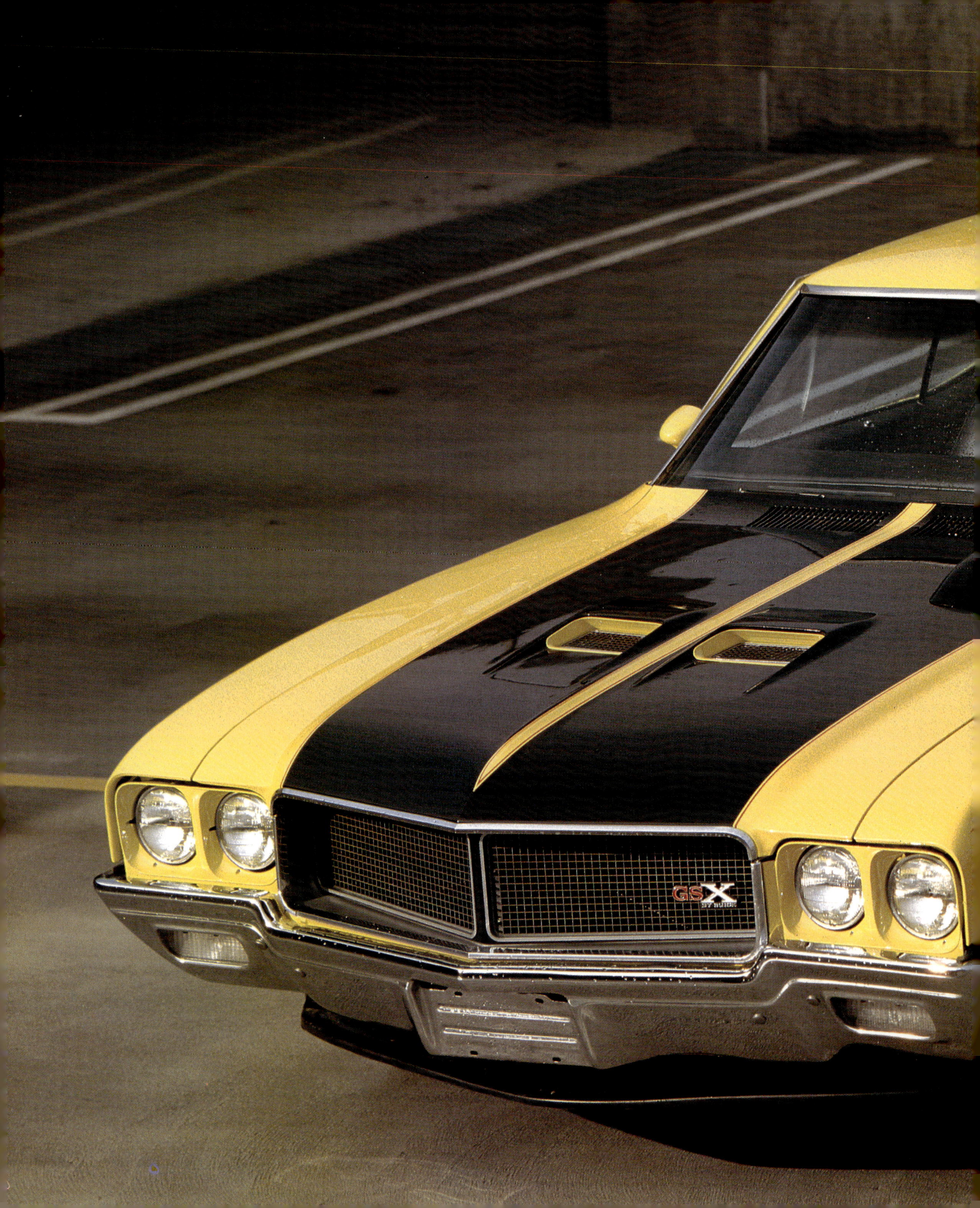
GSX

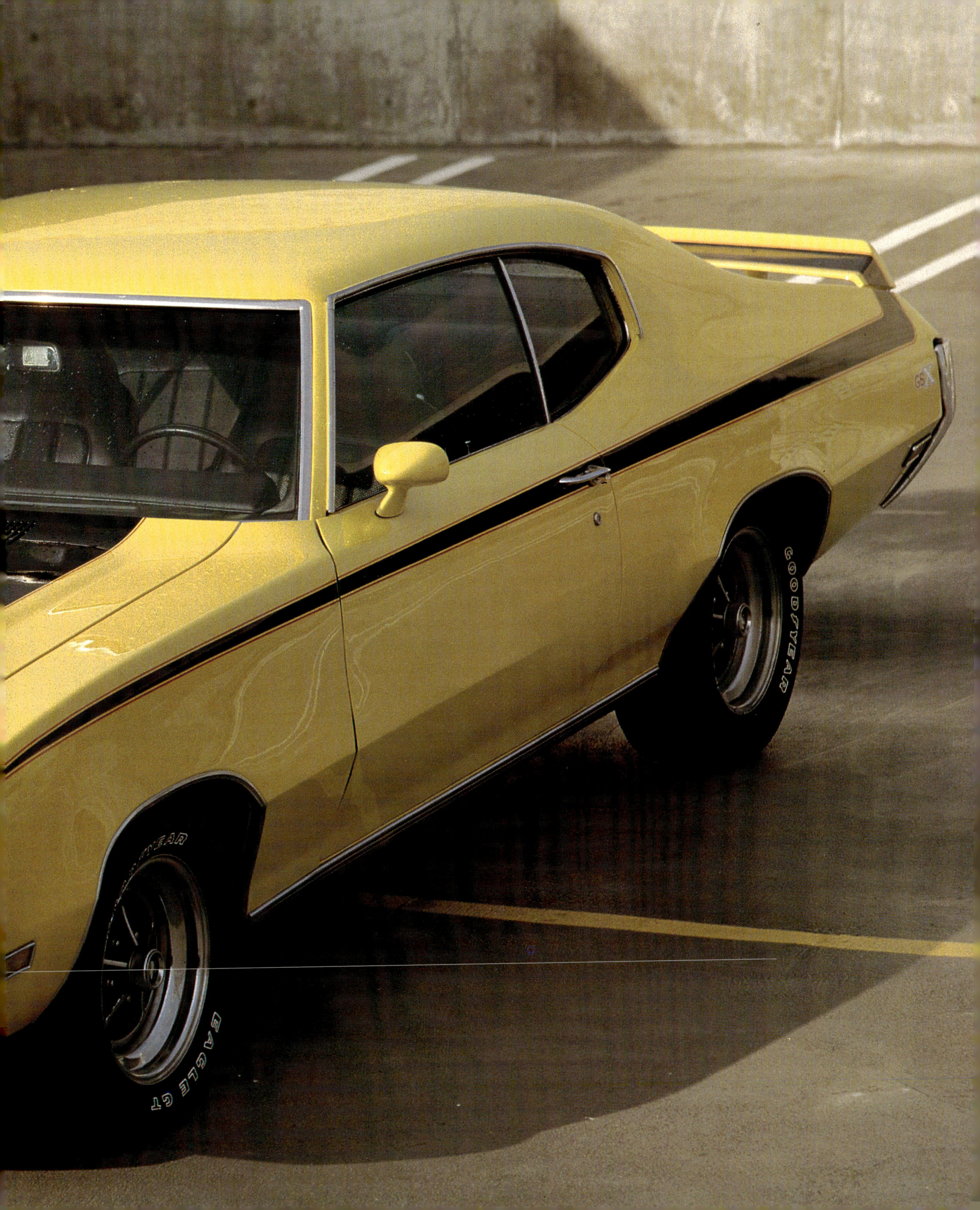
GSX
GOODYEAR
EAGLE GT

*B*uick's potent GSX was available in two colors only—Apollo White and Saturn Yellow. Both carried the decorative black and red striping accents, and both sported the black interior option. The rear spoiler—on the chapter opening page—was fiberglass. Also part of the package was a front air dam. In the picture on the previous page, this aerodynamic aid can be seen protruding just below the bumper. Pictured here, a bird's-eye view of the front end of the GSX. On the left side of the hood, right in the driver's line of vision, was the exterior tachometer, which was included in the GSX package. The distinctive hood scoops were, indeed, functional and part of an induction system Buick called Cool Air. The photograph above shows the underhood scene. Prominently visible are the twin funnels that connect the scoops with the double-snorkel air cleaner. The side view on the following page stands as proof of the exciting package designed by Buick stylists using relatively simple touches.

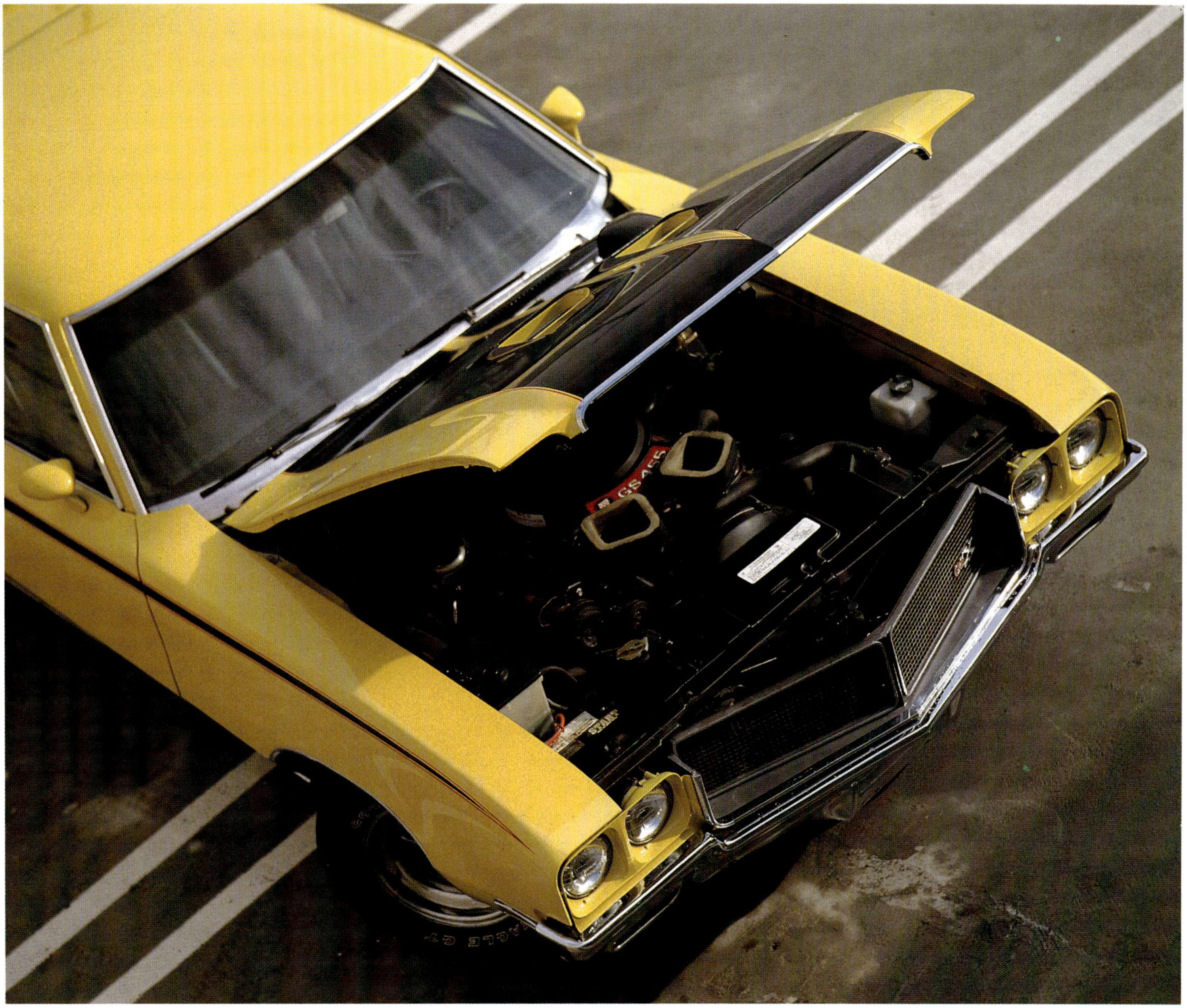
GS455

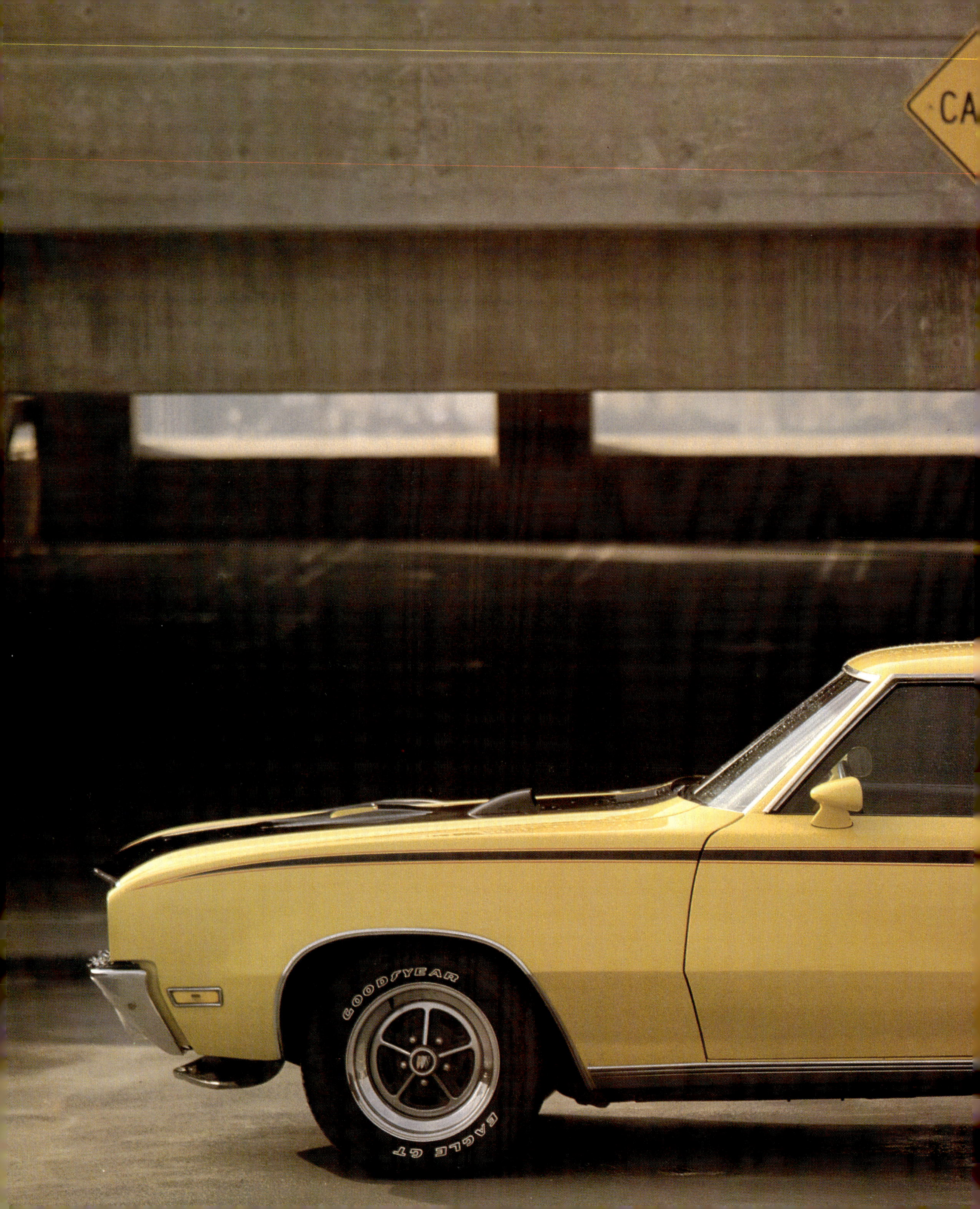
CA
GOODYEAR
EAGLE GT

5 MPH

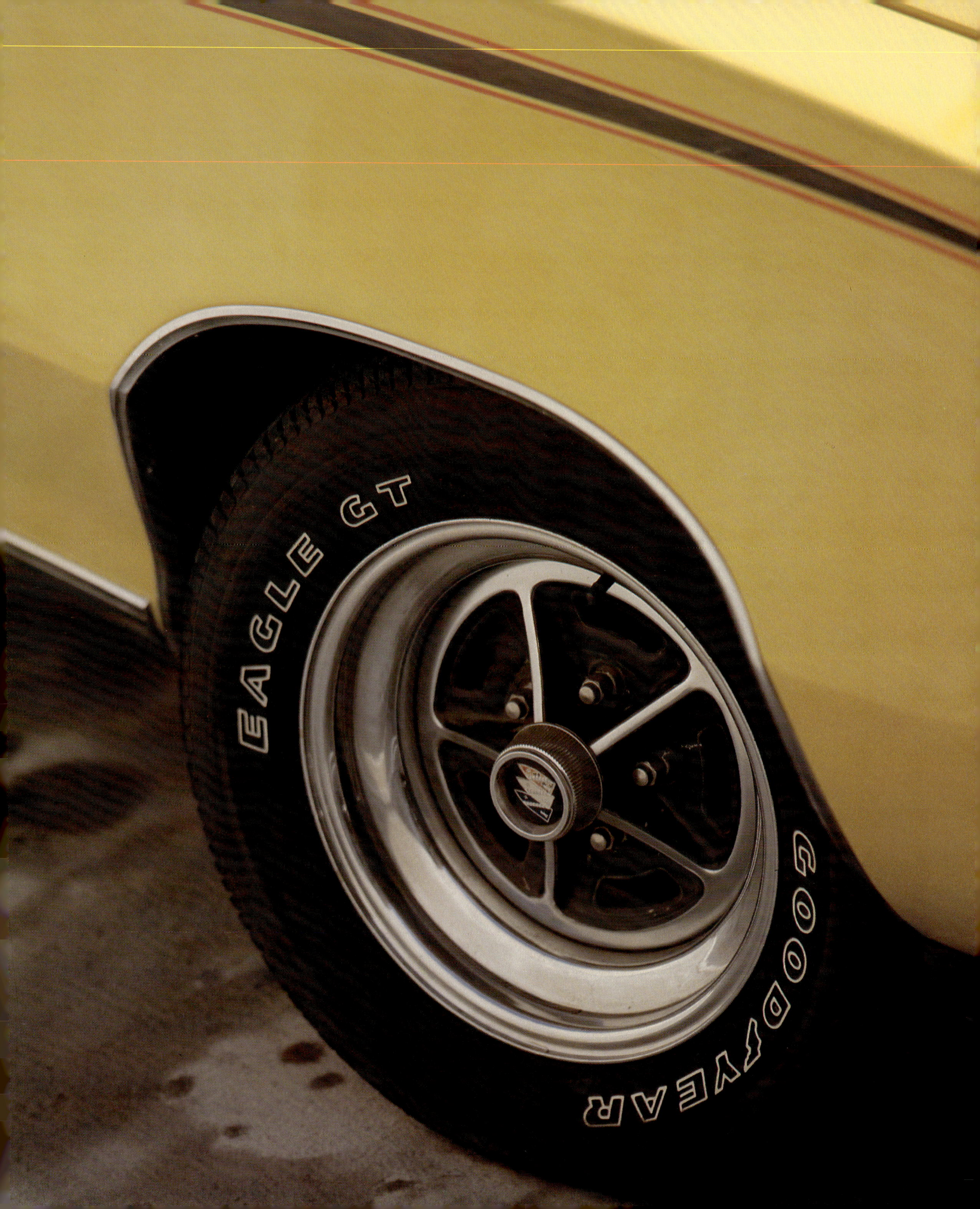
EAGLE GT
GOODYEAR

The GSX rolled on seven-inch-wide, five-spoked chrome wheels—to the left. The interior of the package featured all-vinyl, custom-padded buckets. Adding to the luxurious atmosphere were such amenities as power seats, tilt wheel, power windows and air conditioning. All these items added weight, and, measuring over 4,000 pounds at the curb, it was a miracle that the GSX performed so phenomenally well—in stock configuration, the machine was capable of covering the quarter-mile in less than 14 seconds. The particular example featured on these pages has been driven daily since new by its first and present owner, and is fitted with the optional console-mounted lever that connects to a three-speed automatic. A four-speed manual with a Hurst linkage was standard. The attractive steering wheel—above— was also standard Gran Sport fare. The entire GSX package cost just over $5,000.

1971 Chevrolet Chevelle SS LS-6

Last of the big-blocks turns lean

Chevelle hangs out at Orange County Raceway.

The Chevelle, Chevrolet's mid-size entry, arrived in 1964. The SS version, which stood for Super Sport, should have been a performance machine—but it was not. Although hyped as such in advertising, potential buyers found it to be nothing more than a trim option in the Malibu line.

Standard power on these early Chevelles consisted of a 120 hp six and a 195 hp eight. Bucket seats, special instrumentation, deluxe steering wheel, floor-mounted console panel and optional tachometer were trimmings that added up to an attractive package. Power, however, was lacking.

In 1965, among other minor styling changes, came a new grille. While the standard engines remained the same, there were some interesting additions among the options: the 327 ci V-8 in a 250 hp, a 300 hp or a 350 hp configuration.

Then, in early 1965, came the classic combination—the original big-block 396 ci, option RPO L37, producing 375 hp and fitted to a lightened body, created the RPO Z16—reproduced just 200 times, plus one in convertible guise.

Chevrolet saw these machines mainly as public relations tools—used as demonstrators and test cars, and for executive transportation—very few reached the drag strips. The few that did scored quarter-mile times in the mid-fourteen range. But the mere existence of these very special Chevelles lent luster to the future siblings of the line.

For 1966, there was new styling, with two simulated hood scoops. Available in both coupe and convertible versions, power came from the detuned 396 Turbo-Jet, producing 325 hp. The changes for 1967 were minor, with the Turbo-Jet available also in a 350 hp variation.

The Chevelle received a major re-styling in 1968, adopting the corporate shape shared with other marques in the General Motors brotherhood. The new body had a longer hood and a shorter rear. The SS 396 was still a separate series, with coupe and convertible models. Power remained unchanged. Although not documented in sales figures, it is thought that the potent 396 was placed in about 2,000 units that year.

For 1969, the Chevelle again became an option package rather than a separate series—a Malibu provided the base. Again, power was unchanged but, once more, a limited-edition issue is said to have been available, featuring the awesome 425 hp 427, borrowed from the Corvette line. Five hundred such Chevelles are thought to have been built.

In 1970 came the big-block climax—the Chevelle could be ordered with the LS-6 option, which featured the 396 stroked to its biggest bore, 454 ci. In this guise 450 hp was extracted. Many consider this machine to be the most outstanding chassis and powertrain combination of the era. Just 3,733 Chevelles were equipped with the LS-6 option that year.

The following year, 1971, saw the last of the muscle car Chevelles—and the beginning of the decline. The LS-6 option was still available, but the compression ratio had been cut from 10.25 to 8.5, and the huge 454 managed "only" 365 hp. Still, it was a last hurrah with a lot of gusto.

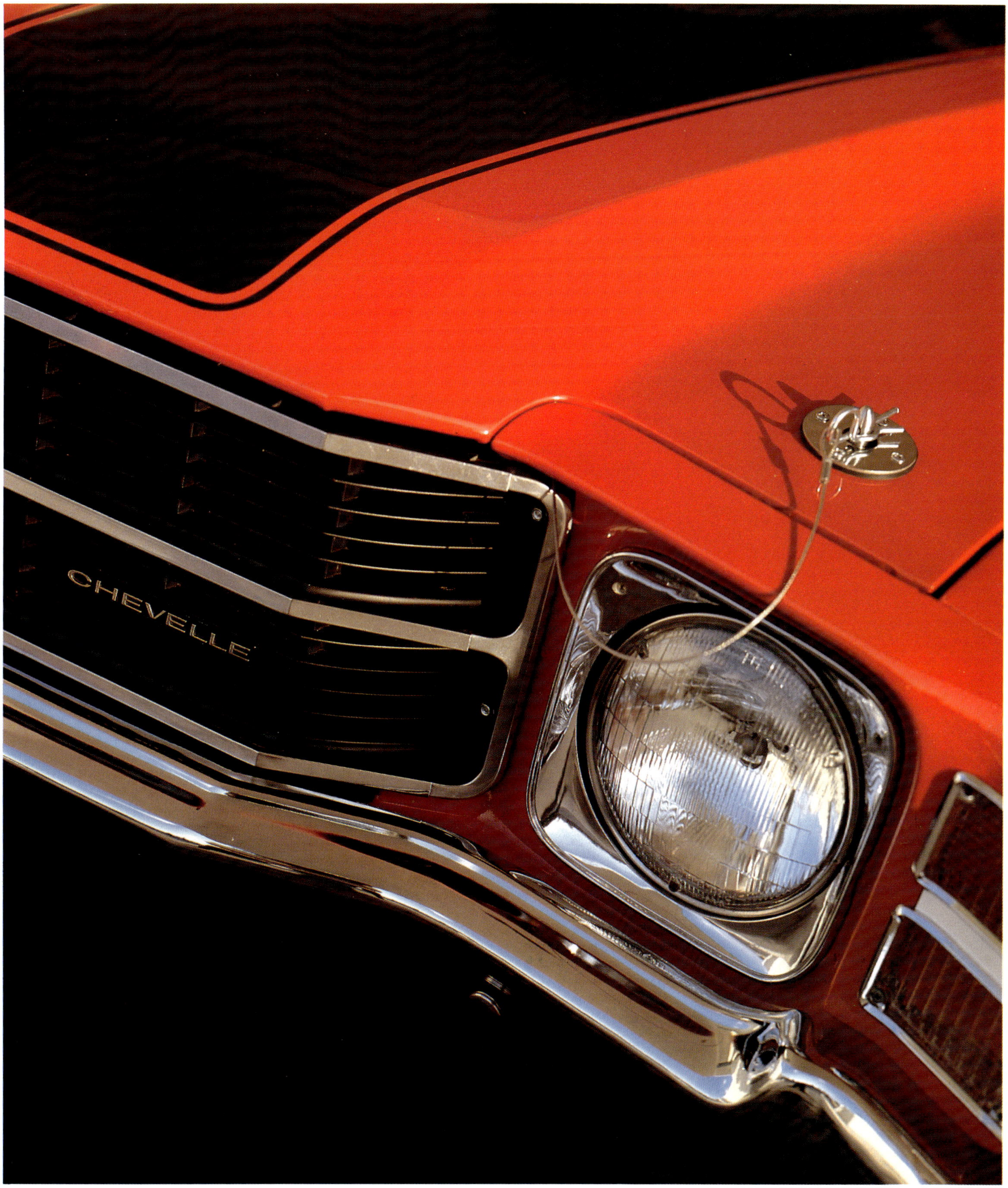
CHEVELLE

The Chevelle went through a series of transformations, some more radical than others. The example featured on these pages shows the 1971 look, which constituted a minor adjustment of the basic style introduced in 1968. In order to end up with a Chevelle SS LS-6, one had to be something of a wizard at reading the sales literature. The buyer had to start with a Malibu coupe, add the SS 454 option, and top it all off with the LS-6 option—somewhat like adding frosting on top of frosting. In its 1971 form, the Chevelle was true to the original muscle car concept—a big engine in a medium-size body. Although the Malibu had gained additional pounds, the engine was still supremely big, so that the contrast remained. Also true to the basic concept, the Chevelle, in spite of the giant it housed under the hood, still had the basic appearance of an average car. Then again, who are we kidding? With the big wheels and the stripes, even Grandma would have known something was different.

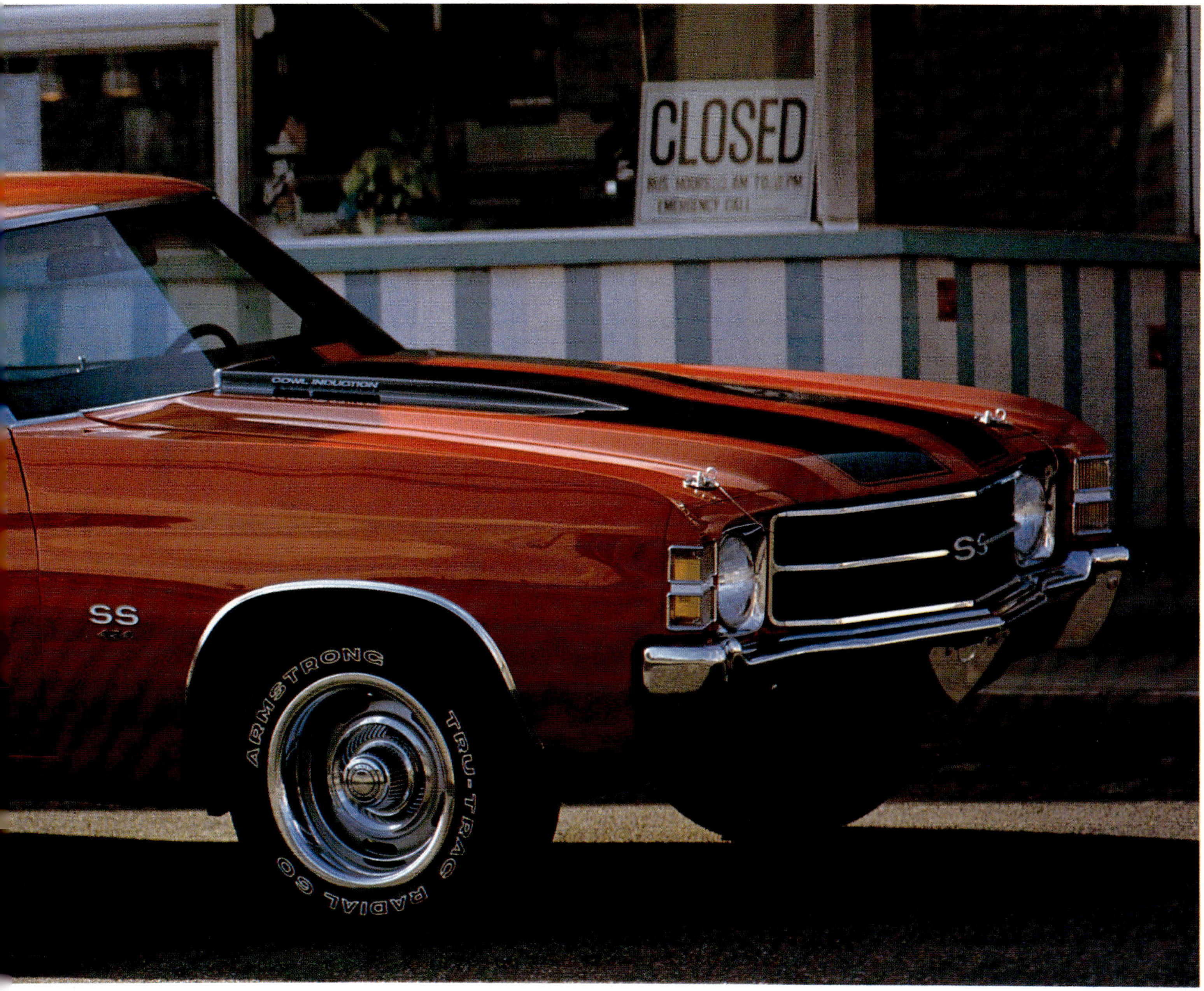
CLOSED
COWL INDUCTION
SS
ARMSTRONG
TRU-TRAC
RADIAL 60

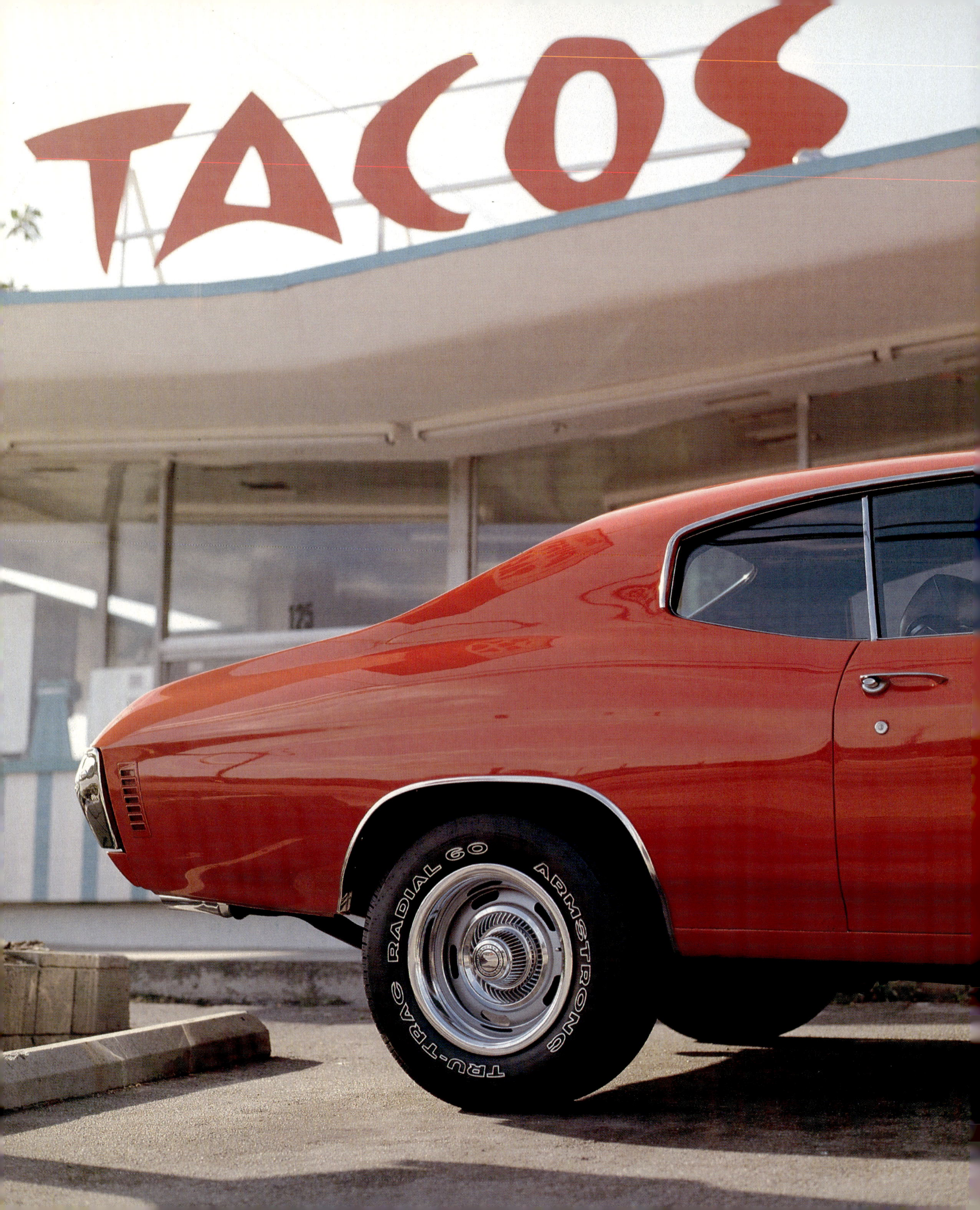
TACOS
125
RADIAL 60
ARMSTRONG
TRU-TRAC

Equally at home in the driveway of a taco stand and on the tarmac of a drag strip, the Chevelle cut an impressive figure, exuding competence from every angle. Details made the difference between the Chevelle models of various years. For 1971, having used twin headlights since its inception, the Chevelle received single Power-Beam units, on the opening pages of the chapter. Also new for this year were the twin taillights, above. The owners of the outstanding example featured on these pages specialize in automotive detailing. In the following picture, the result of their effort is accentuated by the color-enhancing light of the setting sun. The wheels are the wide seven-inch Rallye option. Beyond the rims hide 11 inch discs up front and 9.5 inch drums in the back. Contemporary road testers generally praised the brakes, finding them more than adequate for the Chevelle's high level of performance.

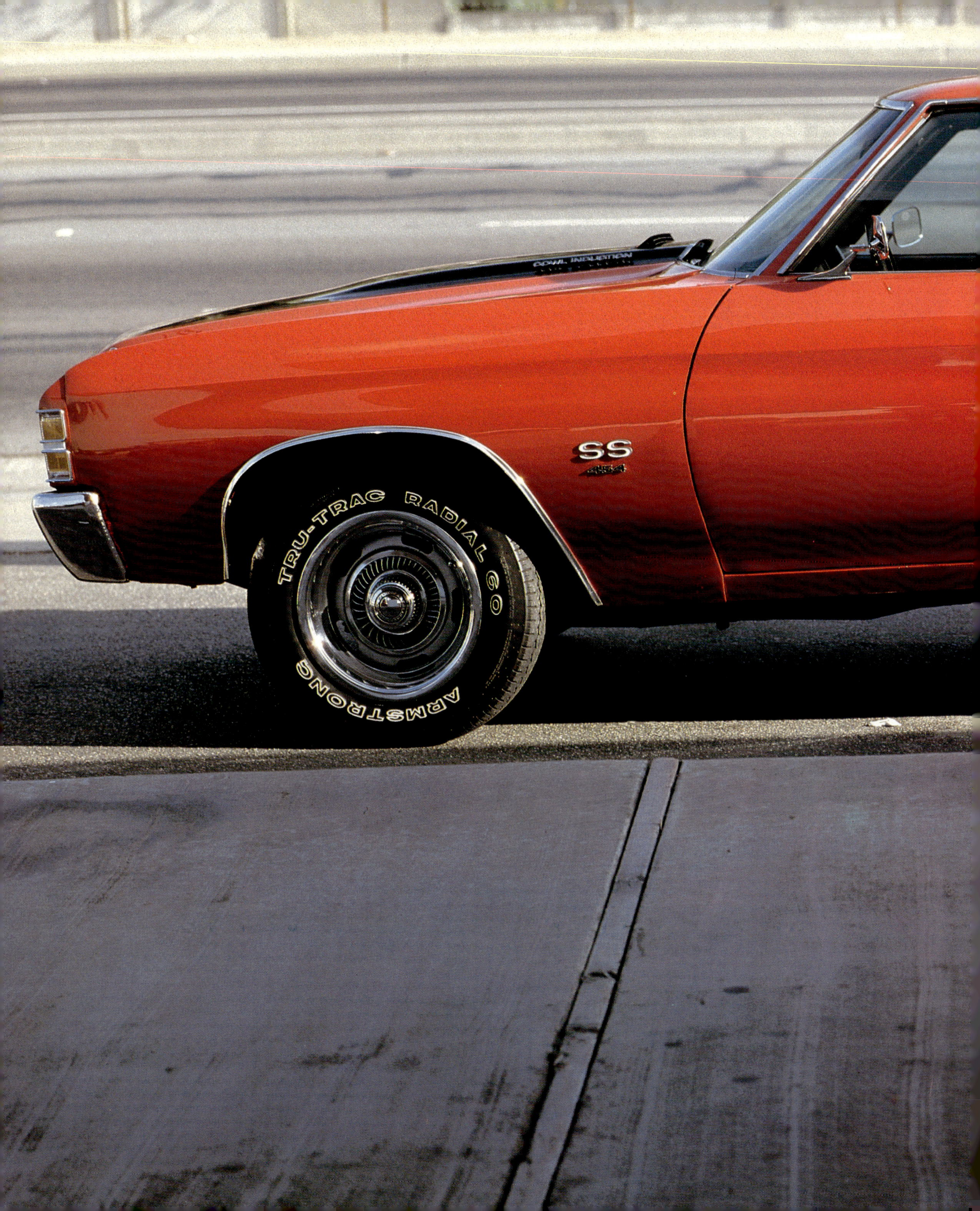
COWL INDUCTION
SS
TRU-TRAC RADIAL 60
ARMSTRONG

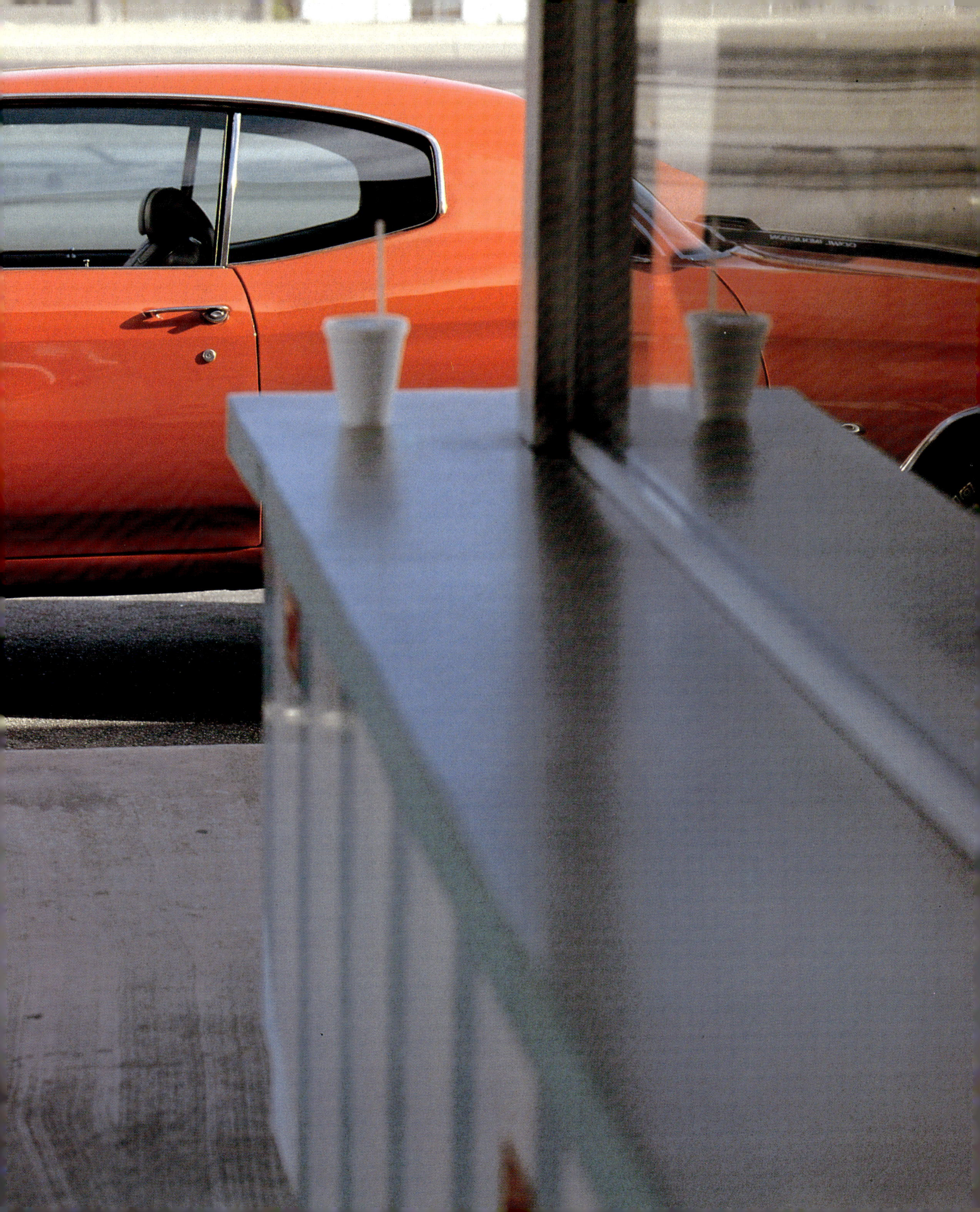

Above, an engine compartment restored to perfection—as flawless today as it was when the car rolled off the showroom floor. Featured in the photograph to the right, the 14 inch padded steering wheel was also new for 1971, and part of a $100 appearance option. Also included in this package was a complete assortment of gauges, with the tachometer and the speedometer flanking the steering column. On the following page, a close-up of the exterior manifestations of the Chevelle's optional cowl induction system. The visible elements consisted of the lettering and the flap. Vacuum operated, the flap stayed open only when the engine was turned off or when it was operated at full throttle. Not visible from the outside was the open top of the air cleaner, and the soft rubber ring that facilitated the sealing between the valve and the hood. Cowl induction was probably more of a gimmick than an actual boost to performance, at least at lower speeds.

The author wishes to thank Bob Brennan, Don Emmons, Dennis Graham, Mike Laugen, Chip Miller and Ron Rotter for providing leads to the featured cars as well as valuable research material. Also, appreciation is extended to the owners of the stars of the book, Ty Froemke—Bel Air; Jerry Moreland—Max Wedge (restored by Bob Bauder), Thunderbolt, Superbird; Rod Folsom—GTO, Firebird; Pete Haldiman—Satellite, Challenger; Vintage Auto Collections (Otis Chandler and Greg Joseph)—Camaro; George Boskovich, Jr.—Mustang; Herb Gleicke—Buick (restored by Gary Nelson and Alan Rodrigues); and Robert and Marcia Baumann—Chevelle.